SARA L. WESTON

From Battlefields to Thrones: The Empowered Women of Celtic Lore and History

Copyright © 2023 by Sara L. Weston

All rights reserved. No part of this publication may be reproduced, stored or transmitted in any form or by any means, electronic, mechanical, photocopying, recording, scanning, or otherwise without written permission from the publisher. It is illegal to copy this book, post it to a website, or distribute it by any other means without permission.

Sara L. Weston asserts the moral right to be identified as the author of this work.

Sara L. Weston has no responsibility for the persistence or accuracy of URLs for external or third-party Internet Websites referred to in this publication and does not guarantee that any content on such Websites is, or will remain, accurate or appropriate.

Designations used by companies to distinguish their products are often claimed as trademarks. All brand names and product names used in this book and on its cover are trade names, service marks, trademarks and registered trademarks of their respective owners. The publishers and the book are not associated with any product or vendor mentioned in this book. None of the companies referenced within the book have endorsed the book.

First edition

This book was professionally typeset on Reedsy.
Find out more at reedsy.com

Contents

Preface

"From Battlefields to Thrones: The Empowered Women of Celtic Lore and History" is a remarkable journey into the heart of a culture often shrouded in myth and mystery. Through the pages of this book, we embark on a quest to unveil the hidden stories of Celtic women, those whose voices have been marginalized and underestimated by the annals of history. With each chapter, we bring these women out of the shadows and into the spotlight, where they rightfully belong.

Celtic societies have long captured the imagination of the world with their enchanting legends and storied past. Yet, amidst the tales of heroic warriors and mystical druids, the remarkable role of women has too often been relegated to the footnotes of history. In "From Battlefields to Thrones," we endeavor to rectify this historical oversight. This book seeks to reveal the strength and resilience of Celtic women, who actively participated in warfare, held positions of power, and were integral to the cultural tapestry of the Celtic world.

We delve into the past, examining historical accounts, mythological tales, and archaeological discoveries that offer evidence of female warriors and leaders. Through the lens of history and archaeology, we uncover the stories of women like Boudica (Boadicea) and Queen Medb (Maeve), whose indomitable spirits left an indelible mark on their people and their time.

But this book is not just a chronicle of warriors. It delves deeper into Celtic mythology, where we find the presence of powerful female figures, including the Morrígan and other warrior goddesses who loom large in Celtic culture. It explores their significance in shaping beliefs about war and battle. Beyond the battlefield, we also explore the broader roles of women in Celtic society, shedding light on their contributions to politics, leadership, and the economy.

In the course of our exploration, we critically examine the patriarchal lens through which history and archaeology have often been written. We challenge biases and misconceptions, reevaluate artifacts and burial practices, and emphasize the transformative impact of unveiling these hidden histories. Moreover, we take a closer look at the concept of gender fluidity in Celtic cultures and its cultural significance, offering valuable insights for our own modern society.

1

Chapter 1

Overview:

From Battlefields to Thrones: The Empowered Women of Celtic Lore and History is a groundbreaking exploration of the often overlooked and underestimated role of women in Celtic societies. This book delves into the evidence that suggests Celtic women actively participated in warfare and held positions of power. Through a comprehensive analysis of historical accounts, mythological tales, and archaeological findings, it sheds light on the remarkable stories of female warriors and leaders, including Boudica (Boadicea) and Queen Medb (Maeve).

The book also delves into Celtic mythology, highlighting the presence of powerful female figures such as the Morrígan and other warrior goddesses. It examines their significance in Celtic culture and their association with war and battle. Furthermore, it explores the broader roles of women in Celtic society beyond warfare, including their contributions to politics, leadership, and the economy.

In addition to uncovering the hidden histories of Celtic women, this book critically examines the patriarchal lens through which history and archaeology have often been written. It challenges biases and misconceptions, reevaluates artifacts and burial practices, and highlights the impact of unveiling these hidden histories. Moreover, it explores the concept of gender fluidity in Celtic cultures and its cultural significance, offering valuable lessons for modern society.

Overall, "From Battlefield to Thrones" provides a comprehensive and thought-provoking account of the remarkable contributions and experiences of Celtic women. It aims to inspire modern readers, shed light on the influence of Celtic warrior women on feminist movements, and emphasize the importance of recognizing and celebrating women's contributions throughout history.

Introduction to Celtic Societies and Gender Roles

1.1 Overview of Celtic Societies

Celtic societies, which flourished during the Iron Age in Europe, were known for their rich cultural traditions, intricate artwork, and complex social structures. These societies were spread across a vast region, including present-day Ireland, Scotland, Wales, and parts of France and Germany. The Celts were a diverse group of people with distinct regional variations, but they shared common linguistic and cultural characteristics.

Celtic societies were organized into tribes or clans, led by chieftains or kings who held political and military power. These societies were predominantly agrarian, with a strong emphasis on cattle farming and agriculture. The Celts had a hierarchical social structure, with warriors and nobles occupying the highest positions, followed by farmers, craftsmen, and slaves.

The Celts had a strong warrior culture, and warfare played a significant role in their society. They engaged in inter-tribal conflicts, territorial disputes, and raids on neighboring communities. The Celts were renowned for their skilled warriors, who were highly respected and held in high regard within their communities.

While the role of men as warriors in Celtic societies is well-documented, there is growing evidence to suggest that women also played active roles in warfare and held positions of power. The patriarchal lens through which history and archaeology have often been written may have downplayed or ignored the different roles of women in Celtic societies. However, recent research and discoveries have shed light on the significant contributions of women in Celtic warfare and leadership.

Archaeological evidence, such as grave goods and weaponry found in burial sites, suggests that women were buried with weapons and armor, indicating their involvement in warfare. For example, the burial site of a woman in Vix, France, contained a chariot and a bronze cauldron, symbolizing her high status and potential military role. Similarly, the discovery of female skeletons with injuries consistent with combat suggests that women actively participated in battles.

In Celtic mythology, there are several female figures associated with war and battle. One prominent example is the Morrígan, a goddess of war and sovereignty. She is often depicted as a fierce warrior, shape-shifter, and prophetess who played a crucial role in determining the outcome of battles. Other warrior goddesses, such as Macha and Badb, were also revered for their martial prowess and were believed to inspire and protect warriors in battle.

Historical accounts also provide evidence of female warriors in Celtic societies. Boudica, also known as Boadicea, was a warrior queen who led a rebellion against the Roman Empire in 60-61 CE. Her military campaigns and leadership skills demonstrated the significant role women could play in Celtic warfare. Queen Medb, a legendary figure in Irish mythology, was another powerful female leader who played a central role in the epic tale of Táin Bó Cúailnge (The Cattle Raid of Cooley). Medb's portrayal as a strong and assertive queen highlights the existence of women in positions of authority in Celtic societies.

The existence of women warriors in Celtic societies challenges the traditional gender roles assigned to women in ancient societies. It suggests that Celtic women had agency and were not confined to domestic roles alone. The importance of gender fluidity in Celtic cultures cannot be overlooked. Celtic societies had a more fluid understanding of gender, where individuals could embody both masculine and feminine qualities. This fluidity allowed women to participate in traditionally male-dominated activities, including warfare and leadership.

The recognition of women's contributions in Celtic societies is not only important for understanding the past but also for inspiring and empowering women today. By uncovering the hidden histories of warrior women, we can challenge patriarchal biases and promote a more inclusive understanding of history. The cultural significance of gender fluidity in Celtic societies serves as a reminder that gender roles are not fixed and can be reimagined in contemporary society.

In the following chapters, we will delve deeper into the lives and legacies of specific warrior women in Celtic societies, examining their historical backgrounds, leadership abilities, and impact on Celtic women. We will also explore the role of women in Celtic mythology and the broader cultural significance of gender fluidity. Through this exploration, we hope to shed light on the often-overlooked contributions of women in Celtic societies and inspire a reevaluation of gender roles in our own time.

1.2 Gender Roles in Celtic Societies

Celtic societies were complex and diverse, with a rich tapestry of cultural practices and beliefs. In order to understand the role of women in these societies, it is important to examine the prevailing gender roles and expectations. While it is true that Celtic societies were predominantly patriarchal, with men holding positions of power and authority, there is evidence to suggest that women also played significant roles, including participating in warfare and holding positions of power.

1.2.1 Women in Celtic Society: A Multifaceted Role

In Celtic societies, women held multifaceted roles that extended beyond the domestic sphere. They were not merely confined to the roles of wives and mothers, but actively participated in various aspects of community life. Women were involved in agriculture, animal husbandry, and craft production, contributing to the economic well-being of their communities. They were skilled in weaving, pottery, and metalwork, and their craftsmanship was highly valued.

Furthermore, women in Celtic societies had a voice in decision-making processes. They participated in community gatherings and had the ability to influence the outcome of important decisions. This suggests that women held a certain level of social and political agency within their communities.

1.2.2 Women Warriors in Celtic Mythology

Celtic mythology provides us with a glimpse into the cultural beliefs and values of the ancient Celts. In these mythological tales, we find numerous examples of powerful and fierce female figures associated with war and battle. One such figure is the Morrígan, the goddess of war and battle. She is often depicted as a shape-shifter, appearing as a crow or raven, and is known for her prophetic abilities and her role in guiding warriors into battle.

Other warrior goddesses in Celtic mythology include Macha, who was associated with sovereignty and war, and Badb, who was associated with battle and death. These mythological figures highlight the cultural significance of female warriors in Celtic societies and suggest that women were not only respected but also revered for their martial prowess.

1.2.3 Historical Accounts of Women Warriors

Beyond mythology, there are historical accounts that provide evidence of women warriors in Celtic societies. One notable example is Boudica, also known as Boadicea, the warrior queen of the Iceni tribe in ancient Britain. Boudica led a rebellion against the Roman occupation in the 1st century CE, demonstrating her military leadership and strategic prowess. Her actions challenged the Roman forces and inspired her people to fight for their freedom.

Another prominent figure is Queen Medb, also known as Maeve, from Irish mythology. While her historical existence is debated, she is depicted as a powerful and assertive queen who led her armies in the Táin Bó Cúailnge (The Cattle Raid of

Cooley). Medb's role as a warrior queen challenges the notion that women were passive participants in Celtic warfare.

1.2.4 Challenging Patriarchal Biases in History and Archaeology

The patriarchal lens through which history and archaeology have often been written has led to the downplaying or outright erasure of women's roles in Celtic societies. The focus on male warriors and leaders has overshadowed the contributions and achievements of women. However, recent research and reevaluation of historical and archaeological evidence have begun to shed light on the diverse roles of women in Celtic societies.

Archaeological discoveries, such as the presence of weapons and armor in female burials, suggest that women actively participated in warfare. The discovery of female warriors buried with their weapons challenges the assumption that warfare was exclusively a male domain. These findings indicate that women not only fought alongside men but also held positions of authority within their communities.

1.2.5 Gender Fluidity in Celtic Cultures

Celtic cultures exhibited a certain degree of gender fluidity, which is the recognition and acceptance of gender identities beyond the traditional binary of male and female. The existence of third gender roles, such as the Gaulish and Irish "berdache," suggests that Celtic societies had a more nuanced understanding of gender.

The berdache were individuals who did not conform to traditional gender norms and were often associated with spiritual and magical practices. They were considered to possess both masculine and feminine qualities and were respected for their unique perspectives and abilities. This acceptance of gender fluidity challenges the rigid gender roles imposed by patriarchal societies and highlights the cultural significance of embracing diverse gender identities.

Conclusion

In conclusion, while Celtic societies were predominantly patriarchal, evidence suggests that women played significant roles beyond the domestic sphere. Women participated in warfare, held positions of power and authority, and contributed to the economic and cultural well-being of their communities. The presence of female warriors in Celtic mythology and the archaeological evidence of women buried with weapons challenge the patriarchal biases in historical and archaeological research. Furthermore, the recognition of gender fluidity in Celtic cultures highlights the cultural significance of embracing diverse gender identities. By uncovering and celebrating the hidden histories of Celtic women, we can challenge patriarchal biases and gain a deeper understanding of the rich and complex tapestry of Celtic societies.

1.3 Patriarchal Lens in History and Archaeology

Throughout history, the lens through which history and archaeology have been written has often been influenced by patriarchal biases. This has resulted in the downplaying or even complete erasure of the different roles and contributions of women in

Celtic societies. By examining the evidence and challenging these biases, we can begin to unveil the hidden histories of warrior women in Celtic cultures.

1.3.1 Historical Biases and Misrepresentations

The patriarchal lens through which history has been written has often led to the marginalization of women's roles in society, including their participation in warfare. Traditional historical accounts have predominantly focused on male warriors, leaders, and political figures, while neglecting the stories and achievements of women. This has created a distorted narrative that perpetuates the notion that women were passive and confined to domestic roles.

Archaeology, too, has been influenced by these biases. The interpretation of artifacts and burial practices has often been skewed towards reinforcing traditional gender roles, with assumptions made about the roles and status of individuals based on their gender. This has resulted in the misidentification or misrepresentation of women's roles in Celtic societies.

1.3.2 Challenging the Narrative: Evidence of Women Warriors

Despite the patriarchal lens, there is evidence to suggest that Celtic women did participate in warfare and held positions of power in some cases. Historical accounts and mythological tales provide glimpses into the lives of female warriors who defied societal expectations and played active roles in battles and leadership.

One prominent example is Boudica, also known as Boadicea, the warrior queen of the Iceni tribe in ancient Britain. Boudica led a rebellion against the Roman Empire in the 1st century CE, demonstrating her military prowess and strategic leadership. Her story challenges the notion that women were solely confined to domestic roles and highlights the existence of powerful female figures in Celtic societies.

In Irish mythology, Queen Medb, also known as Maeve, is another example of a powerful female figure. Medb is depicted as a fierce warrior queen who led her armies in the legendary Táin Bó Cúailnge (The Cattle Raid of Cooley). Her role as a military leader and her ability to command respect and loyalty from her warriors challenges the traditional narrative of women's roles in Celtic societies.

Celtic mythology is rich with female figures associated with war and battle. The Morrígan, a goddess of war and sovereignty, is often depicted as a shape-shifter who appears on the battlefield to inspire warriors. Other warrior goddesses, such as Macha and Badb, also play significant roles in Celtic mythology. These mythological tales provide further evidence of the cultural acceptance and recognition of women's participation in warfare.

1.3.3 Unveiling Hidden Histories: Reevaluating the Evidence

To uncover the hidden histories of warrior women in Celtic societies, it is crucial to reevaluate the evidence with a critical eye and challenge the assumptions and biases that have shaped historical and archaeological interpretations.

Reexamining artifacts and burial practices can provide valuable insights into the roles and status of women in Celtic societies. By analyzing grave goods and burial contexts, researchers can identify indicators of warrior status, such as weapons, armor, and symbols of power. Recent archaeological discoveries have revealed the presence of such indicators in female burials, suggesting that women held positions of authority and participated in warfare.

Additionally, the reinterpretation of historical accounts and mythological tales can shed light on the contributions and achievements of women. By examining these narratives through a gender-inclusive lens, we can uncover the stories of warrior women that have been overlooked or dismissed in traditional interpretations.

1.3.4 The Importance of Gender Fluidity in Celtic Cultures

Celtic cultures exhibited a remarkable degree of gender fluidity, challenging the binary understanding of gender roles that has often been imposed by patriarchal societies. The existence of female warriors and leaders in Celtic societies suggests a more fluid and inclusive understanding of gender, where individuals were not confined to rigid gender expectations.

The acceptance and recognition of gender fluidity in Celtic cultures had significant cultural and social implications. It allowed for a more equitable distribution of power and authority, enabling women to participate in warfare and hold positions of leadership. This cultural significance of gender fluidity in Celtic societies challenges the notion that gender roles are fixed and highlights the potential for greater gender equality in modern society.

By exploring the hidden histories of warrior women in Celtic societies and understanding the importance of gender fluidity, we can challenge the patriarchal biases that have shaped histor-ical and archaeological narratives. This reevaluation allows us to recognize and celebrate the diverse roles and contributions of women in Celtic cultures, inspiring us to question and challenge gender norms in our own society.

1.4 Importance of Gender Fluidity in Celtic Cultures

Gender fluidity refers to the concept that gender is not fixed and can change over time or in different contexts. In Celtic cultures, gender fluidity played a significant role in shaping societal norms and expectations. Understanding the importance of gender fluidity in Celtic cultures is crucial for challenging patriarchal biases and unveiling the hidden histories of warrior women.

1.4.1 Fluidity in Gender Roles

Celtic societies had a more fluid understanding of gender roles compared to many other ancient civilizations. While there were certainly expectations and divisions based on gender, these roles were not rigidly defined. Men and women had the freedom to engage in various activities and pursue different paths in life.

In Celtic societies, women were not confined to traditional domestic roles. They had the opportunity to participate in warfare, politics, and leadership positions. This fluidity in gender roles allowed women to challenge societal norms and assert their agency in ways that were not always possible in other ancient cultures.

1.4.2 Symbolism in Celtic Mythology

Celtic mythology provides further evidence of the importance of gender fluidity in Celtic cultures. Female figures in Celtic mythology, such as the Morrígan, were associated with war and battle. These goddesses embodied both masculine and feminine qualities, blurring the lines between gender roles.

The Morrígan, for example, was a complex deity who could take on the form of a crow or a beautiful woman. She represented the power and ferocity of battle, challenging the notion that warfare was solely the domain of men. The inclusion of such powerful and multifaceted female figures in Celtic mythology suggests a cultural acceptance of gender fluidity and the recognition of women's potential in traditionally male-dominated spheres.

1.4.3 Social Acceptance and Cultural Significance

The acceptance of gender fluidity in Celtic cultures had profound social and cultural implications. It allowed for a more inclusive and egalitarian society where individuals were not confined by rigid gender norms. This fluidity created space for women to assert their autonomy and contribute to various aspects of Celtic society, including warfare and leadership.

The cultural significance of gender fluidity in Celtic societies is evident in the stories and legends that have been passed down through generations. These tales often feature strong and influential women who challenge societal expectations and play pivotal roles in shaping the course of history. By recognizing and celebrating the contributions of warrior women, Celtic cultures affirmed the value of gender diversity and the importance of embracing all aspects of human potential.

1.4.4 Lessons for Modern Society

The importance of gender fluidity in Celtic cultures extends beyond the historical context. It offers valuable lessons for modern society, where gender roles and expectations continue to shape individuals' lives.

By examining the fluidity of gender roles in Celtic societies, we can challenge the patriarchal biases that have influenced historical narratives and archaeological interpretations. This exploration allows us to uncover the hidden histories of warrior women and recognize their significant contributions to Celtic societies.

Moreover, understanding the cultural significance of gender fluidity in Celtic cultures can inspire us to create more inclusive and accepting societies today. By embracing the diversity of gender identities and challenging traditional gender norms, we can create spaces where individuals are free to express themselves authentically and contribute to society in meaningful ways.

In conclusion, the importance of gender fluidity in Celtic cultures cannot be overstated. It played a crucial role in shaping societal norms, challenging patriarchal biases, and allowing women to participate in warfare and hold positions of power. By recognizing and understanding the fluidity of gender roles in Celtic societies, we can unveil the hidden histories of warrior women and draw valuable lessons for creating more inclusive and accepting societies in the present day.

2

Chapter 2

Boudica (Boadicea): The Warrior Queen

2.1 Historical Background of Boudica

Boudica, also known as Boadicea, is one of the most renowned warrior queens in Celtic history. Her story is a testament to the strength and resilience of Celtic women in the face of Roman oppression. To understand the historical background of Boudica, we must delve into the context of her time and the events that shaped her life.

2.1.1 Celtic Resistance against Roman Rule

During the first century AD, the Roman Empire sought to expand its territories and exert control over the Celtic tribes inhabiting the British Isles. The Romans viewed the Celts as barbarians and sought to subjugate them under their rule. However, the Celtic tribes fiercely resisted Roman domination, leading to numerous conflicts and uprisings.

2.1.2 Boudica's Early Life

Boudica was born into a noble Celtic family, and she grew up in a society that valued bravery and martial prowess. Little is known about her early life, but it is believed that she was married to Prasutagus, the king of the Iceni tribe in what is now modern-day East Anglia, England.

2.1.3 Roman Invasion and the Iceni Rebellion

In 43 AD, the Roman Empire invaded Britain, and over time, they gradually extended their control over the Celtic tribes. However, the Romans' heavy-handed approach and their mistreatment of the Celtic people led to widespread discontent and resistance.

After the death of her husband, Boudica found herself at odds with the Roman authorities. According to historical accounts, the Romans disregarded the rights of the Iceni tribe and seized their lands, leaving Boudica and her daughters in a vulnerable position. This act of aggression became the catalyst for Boudica's rebellion against Roman rule.

2.1.4 Boudica's Leadership and Military Campaigns

Boudica emerged as a charismatic and influential leader, rallying the Celtic tribes to unite against their common enemy. With her fiery speeches and unwavering determination, she inspired her people to take up arms and fight for their freedom.

Under Boudica's leadership, the Celtic forces launched a series of devastating attacks on Roman settlements and military outposts. The rebellion quickly gained momentum, and Boudica's army inflicted heavy casualties on the Roman legions, causing significant humiliation for the empire.

2.1.5 The Fall of Boudica and Her Legacy

Despite her initial successes, Boudica's rebellion ultimately faced defeat at the hands of the Roman forces. The Romans, with their superior military tactics and resources, managed to crush the Celtic uprising. Boudica's final battle took place in what is now known as the Battle of Watling Street, where her forces were decisively defeated.

Although Boudica did not achieve her ultimate goal of driving the Romans out of Britain, her legacy as a fearless warrior queen and symbol of resistance against oppression endured. Her story became an inspiration for future generations, highlighting the strength and courage of Celtic women.

2.1.6 Historical Accounts and Interpretations

It is important to note that the historical accounts of Boudica's life and rebellion were primarily written by Roman historians, such as Tacitus and Cassius Dio. These accounts may have been influenced by a patriarchal lens, which often downplayed or ignored the roles of women in Celtic societies.

However, archaeological evidence, such as the discovery of weapons and fortifications associated with Boudica's rebellion, suggests that Celtic women actively participated in warfare. This challenges the traditional narrative that portrays Celtic women solely as passive figures in society.

By examining the historical context and piecing together the available evidence, we can begin to uncover the hidden histories of Celtic women like Boudica and shed light on their significant contributions to their societies.

In the next section, we will delve deeper into Boudica's leadership and military campaigns, exploring the strategies she employed and the impact she had on Celtic women.

2.2 Boudica's Leadership and Military Campaigns

Boudica, also known as Boadicea, is one of the most renowned warrior queens in Celtic history. Her leadership and military campaigns have left a lasting impact on Celtic women and continue to inspire generations. In this section, we will delve into the historical background of Boudica, explore her remarkable leadership skills, and examine the military campaigns she led.

Historical Background of Boudica

Boudica was born in the first century AD, during a time when the Roman Empire was expanding its influence across Europe. She belonged to the Iceni tribe, a Celtic tribe located in what is now modern-day East Anglia, England. Boudica's husband, Prasutagus, was the ruler of the Iceni, and upon his death, the Romans attempted to annex the Iceni lands, disregarding the tribe's autonomy.

Boudica's Leadership Skills

Faced with the Roman threat, Boudica emerged as a formidable leader, rallying her people to resist Roman oppression. She possessed exceptional leadership skills, which enabled her to unite various Celtic tribes against their common enemy. Boudica's ability to inspire and mobilize her people is a testament to her charisma and strategic acumen.

Military Campaigns

Boudica's military campaigns were marked by fierce determination and a relentless pursuit of freedom. In 60 or 61 AD, she led a massive uprising against the Roman forces, launching a series of devastating attacks on Roman settlements and military outposts. Her forces, estimated to be in the tens of thousands, inflicted heavy casualties on the Roman legions, causing widespread panic and chaos.

One of the most significant battles led by Boudica was the Battle of Camulodunum (modern-day Colchester). The Roman settlement, which had been established as a colony for retired Roman soldiers, became a target of Boudica's wrath. Her forces razed the city to the ground, leaving a trail of destruction in their wake.

Boudica's military campaigns continued with the sacking of Londinium (modern-day London) and Verulamium (modern-day St. Albans). The Romans were caught off guard by the ferocity and determination of the Celtic forces, and it took considerable effort for them to regain control of the situation.

Boudica's Legacy and Impact on Celtic Women

Boudica's legacy extends far beyond her military campaigns. She became a symbol of resistance and defiance against Roman oppression, inspiring future generations of Celtic women to challenge societal norms and fight for their rights. Boudica's leadership and courage shattered the notion that women were incapable of leading armies or participating in warfare.

Her story serves as a reminder that Celtic women possessed agency and played active roles in their societies. Boudica's example empowered Celtic women to assert themselves and challenge patriarchal structures that sought to confine them to traditional gender roles.

Examining Boudica's Representation in History

Despite Boudica's significant impact, her representation in history has often been overshadowed or distorted by the patriarchal lens through which historical accounts have been written. Many early Roman historians portrayed her as a savage and vengeful warrior, emphasizing her brutality rather than her leadership skills and the justness of her cause.

It is crucial to critically examine historical narratives and question the biases that may have influenced the portrayal of Boudica and other Celtic warrior women. By doing so, we can uncover the hidden histories and challenge the patriarchal biases that have shaped our understanding of Celtic societies.

In the next section, we will explore the mythological accounts of Queen Medb (Maeve), another influential female figure in Celtic history, and uncover the truth behind her myth and reality.

2.3 Boudica's Legacy and Impact on Celtic Women

Boudica, also known as Boadicea, was a remarkable figure in Celtic history and her legacy continues to inspire and empower Celtic women to this day. As a warrior queen, Boudica played a pivotal role in challenging the patriarchal biases of her time and showcasing the strength and resilience of Celtic women. Her impact on Celtic women can be seen in various aspects, from her leadership and military campaigns to her representation in history.

2.3.1 Leadership and Military Campaigns

Boudica's leadership and military campaigns were instrumental in shaping her legacy and inspiring future generations of Celtic women. As the queen of the Iceni tribe, she led a rebellion against the Roman Empire in 60-61 CE, after her tribe was subjected to brutal treatment and her daughters were violated. Boudica's ability to rally her people and lead them into battle demonstrated her exceptional leadership skills and her determination to fight for justice and freedom.

Under Boudica's command, the Celtic forces launched a series of successful attacks against Roman settlements, including the famous sack of Camulodunum (modern-day Colchester). Her military strategies and tactics showcased her strategic prowess and her ability to organize and lead a formidable army. Despite facing overwhelming odds, Boudica's forces managed to inflict heavy casualties on the Roman legions, highlighting the strength and resilience of Celtic warriors, both male and female.

2.3.2 Boudica's Legacy

Boudica's legacy extends far beyond her military campaigns. Her courage and defiance in the face of oppression have made her an enduring symbol of resistance and female empowerment.

Her story has been passed down through generations, inspiring Celtic women to embrace their strength and challenge societal norms.

Boudica's legacy also serves as a reminder of the importance of gender equality and the recognition of women's contributions in Celtic societies. Her leadership and military prowess shattered the notion that women were solely confined to domestic roles and highlighted the potential for women to excel in traditionally male-dominated spheres.

2.3.3 Impact on Celtic Women

Boudica's impact on Celtic women cannot be overstated. Her rebellion against the Roman Empire sent a powerful message to Celtic women, showing them that they too could rise up against oppression and fight for their rights. Boudica's example challenged the prevailing patriarchal biases that sought to confine women to subordinate roles and demonstrated that women were capable of leading armies and shaping the course of history.

Boudica's legacy also inspired Celtic women to assert their agency and challenge societal expectations. Her story served as a catalyst for women to question their own roles and seek greater autonomy and independence. The memory of Boudica's bravery and determination instilled a sense of pride and empowerment among Celtic women, encouraging them to pursue their own ambitions and aspirations.

2.3.4 Examining Boudica's Representation in History

While Boudica's impact on Celtic women is undeniable, it is important to critically examine her representation in history. The patriarchal lens through which history has often been written has led to the downplaying or erasure of women's contributions, including those of Boudica. Historians and archaeologists have often focused on the military aspects of her rebellion, overshadowing her broader significance as a symbol of female empowerment.

By reevaluating Boudica's representation in history, we can uncover the hidden stories and contributions of Celtic women. This reevaluation allows us to challenge the patriarchal biases that have shaped our understanding of Celtic societies and provides a more accurate and inclusive narrative of their history.

Boudica's legacy and impact on Celtic women continue to resonate in modern society. Her story serves as a reminder of the strength and resilience of women throughout history and inspires us to challenge gender norms and fight for equality. By embracing the lessons from Celtic cultures, including the importance of gender fluidity and recognizing women's contributions, we can create a more inclusive and equitable future for all.

2.4 Examining Boudica's Representation in History

Boudica, also known as Boadicea, is one of the most well-known warrior queens in Celtic history. Her story has been passed down through the ages, but it is important to critically examine how she has been represented in history. The patriarchal lens through which history and archaeology have often been written may have downplayed or ignored the different roles of women in Celtic societies, including their participation in warfare and positions of authority. By examining Boudica's representation in history, we can gain a deeper understanding of the challenges faced by warrior women and the biases that have shaped our understanding of their contributions.

2.4.1 Historical Accounts of Boudica

The primary historical accounts of Boudica come from Roman historians, namely Tacitus and Cassius Dio. These accounts were written from a Roman perspective and may have been influenced by their own biases and agendas. It is important to approach these accounts with a critical eye and consider the potential for Roman propaganda and the desire to portray Boudica as a savage and barbaric leader.

2.4.2 Roman Bias and Misrepresentation

The Roman accounts of Boudica often depict her as a vengeful and bloodthirsty warrior, seeking revenge against the Romans for their mistreatment of her and her people. While it is true that Boudica led a rebellion against the Roman occupation of Britain, it is important to question the extent to which her actions were driven by personal vengeance versus a desire for freedom and independence.

The Roman bias against Boudica is evident in the way she is described as a fierce and ruthless leader, leading her people into battle with a thirst for bloodshed. This portrayal serves to reinforce the Roman narrative of the barbaric and uncivilized Celts, while simultaneously downplaying Boudica's strategic military tactics and leadership abilities.

2.4.3 Rediscovering Boudica's Legacy

In recent years, there has been a growing interest in reevaluating Boudica's legacy and challenging the Roman bias that has shaped our understanding of her. Scholars and historians have begun to question the accuracy of the Roman accounts and seek alternative sources of information.

One such alternative source is the archaeological evidence that has been uncovered in Britain. The discovery of burial sites containing weapons and armor traditionally associated with male warriors has raised questions about the role of women in Celtic warfare. Could these burial sites be the final resting place of warrior women like Boudica?

2.4.4 Reevaluating Boudica's Leadership

Another aspect of Boudica's representation in history that deserves reevaluation is her leadership style. The Roman accounts often depict her as a lone warrior, leading her people into battle with little regard for their well-being. However, it is important to consider the cultural context in which Boudica lived and the societal structures that may have influenced her leadership.

Celtic societies were known for their emphasis on communal decision-making and the importance of the collective. It is unlikely that Boudica would have acted unilaterally without the support and input of her people. By reevaluating Boudica's leadership in the context of Celtic society, we can gain a more nuanced understanding of her role as a leader and the strategies she employed to rally her people against the Roman occupation.

2.4.5 Unveiling Boudica's True Legacy

By examining Boudica's representation in history, we can begin to unveil her true legacy as a warrior queen and leader. It is important to recognize the biases that have shaped our understanding of her and to seek out alternative sources of information that challenge the dominant narrative.

Boudica's story serves as a powerful reminder of the strength and resilience of Celtic women in the face of adversity. Her legacy continues to inspire modern women and challenge societal norms. By reclaiming her story and recognizing her contributions, we can begin to rewrite the narrative of Celtic history and give voice to the warrior women who have been overlooked and marginalized.

In the next chapter, we will delve into the mythological accounts of Queen Medb (Maeve) and explore the intersection of myth and reality in understanding the roles of women in Celtic societies.

3

Chapter 3

Queen Medb (Maeve)

3.1 Mythological Accounts of Queen Medb

In Celtic mythology, there are numerous powerful and influential female figures who are associated with war and battle. One such prominent figure is Queen Medb, also known as Maeve. Medb is a complex and multifaceted character whose mythological accounts provide insights into the role of women in Celtic societies.

Medb is primarily known for her role in the epic tale of Táin Bó Cúailnge, also known as The Cattle Raid of Cooley. This ancient Irish saga recounts the conflict between Queen Medb of Connacht and the Ulster hero Cú Chulainn over a prized bull. Medb is depicted as a fierce and determined warrior queen who leads her army into battle with great skill and strategic prowess.

According to the mythological accounts, Medb is portrayed as a strong and independent ruler who is not afraid to challenge societal norms. She is depicted as a charismatic and influential leader who commands the respect and loyalty of her warriors. Medb's role in the Táin Bó Cúailnge highlights her ability to mobilize and lead her forces, demonstrating her authority and power.

Medb's portrayal in Celtic mythology serves as a symbol of female power and authority. She challenges the traditional gender roles and expectations placed upon women in Celtic societies. Medb's character embodies qualities such as bravery, intelligence, and ambition, which are typically associated with male warriors. Her mythological accounts provide evidence of the existence of strong and influential women in Celtic societies who were not confined to traditional gender roles.

It is important to note that while Medb is a mythological figure, her character is believed to be inspired by historical figures and events. The blending of history and mythology in Celtic storytelling makes it challenging to separate fact from fiction. However, the presence of powerful female figures like Medb in Celtic mythology suggests that women held positions of authority and influence in Celtic societies.

In addition to Medb, Celtic mythology is replete with other female warriors and figures associated with war and battle. One such notable figure is the Morrígan, the goddess of war and battle. The Morrígan is often depicted as a shape-shifter who takes the form of a crow or raven and is closely associated with fate and prophecy. She is a formidable and fearsome figure who plays a significant role in Celtic mythological tales.

Other female warriors in Celtic mythology include Scáthach, a warrior queen and skilled martial arts instructor, and Aife, a warrior woman who is said to have been the rival of Scáthach. These mythological accounts further emphasize the existence of powerful and skilled women warriors in Celtic societies.

The representation of female warriors in Celtic mythology challenges the patriarchal biases that have often dominated historical and archaeological research. These mythological accounts provide alternative narratives that highlight the active participation of women in warfare and their positions of power and authority. By examining these mythological accounts, we can begin to unveil the hidden histories of Celtic women and challenge the traditional narratives that have marginalized their contributions.

The significance of gender fluidity in Celtic cultures cannot be overlooked when discussing the roles of women in Celtic societies. Celtic cultures embraced a more fluid understanding of gender, where individuals were not confined to rigid gender roles. This acceptance of gender fluidity allowed women to participate in traditionally male-dominated activities such as warfare and leadership positions. The mythological accounts of female warriors in Celtic societies reflect this cultural acceptance and provide evidence of the diverse roles women played.

In conclusion, the mythological accounts of Queen Medb and other female warriors in Celtic mythology shed light on the active participation of women in warfare and their positions of power and authority. These accounts challenge the patriarchal biases that have often downplayed or ignored the different roles of women in Celtic societies. The importance of gender fluidity in Celtic cultures further emphasizes the cultural significance of women's contributions. By exploring these mythological accounts, we can begin to uncover the hidden histories of Celtic women and recognize their significant impact on society.

3.2 Medb's Role in Táin Bó Cúailnge (The Cattle Raid of Cooley)

In the rich tapestry of Celtic mythology, the figure of Queen Medb (also known as Maeve) stands as a powerful symbol of female authority and leadership. One of the most prominent female figures in Irish mythology, Medb's role in the epic tale of Táin Bó Cúailnge, or The Cattle Raid of Cooley, showcases her prowess as a warrior queen and her determination to assert her power.

3.2.1 The Epic Tale of Táin Bó Cúailnge

Táin Bó Cúailnge is an ancient Irish epic that tells the story of a cattle raid orchestrated by Queen Medb of Connacht. The tale revolves around Medb's desire to possess the prized bull of Cooley, owned by Dáire mac Fiachna. Medb's motivation for the raid is not only driven by her desire for wealth and power but also by her refusal to be outdone by her husband, Ailill, who possesses a bull of equal value.

3.2.2 Medb's Leadership and Military Strategy

Medb's role in Táin Bó Cúailnge is not limited to being a mere instigator of the raid. She actively leads her army into battle, displaying her military prowess and strategic acumen. Medb is depicted as a fearless and skilled warrior, leading her troops with confidence and determination. She is not afraid to take risks and is willing to face any challenge that comes her way.

Throughout the epic, Medb demonstrates her ability to command and inspire her troops. She rallies her warriors, instilling in them a sense of loyalty and determination. Medb's leadership is characterized by her unwavering resolve and her willingness to fight alongside her soldiers, earning their respect and admiration.

3.2.3 Medb's Symbolism of Female Power

Medb's role in Táin Bó Cúailnge goes beyond her military prowess. She symbolizes female power and authority in Celtic mythology. As a queen, Medb holds a position of leadership and influence, challenging the traditional gender roles of her time. Her actions and decisions shape the course of the epic, highlighting the significant role that women played in Celtic societies.

Medb's portrayal as a powerful and independent ruler challenges the patriarchal biases that have often dominated historical narratives. Her character serves as a reminder that women in Celtic societies held positions of authority and were capable of leading armies and making strategic decisions.

3.2.4 Unveiling the Historical Medb

While Medb's character is primarily rooted in mythology, there are indications that she may have been based on a historical figure. The ancient Irish annals mention a queen named Medb who ruled over Connacht during the first century CE. Although the historical accuracy of these accounts is debated, they provide a glimpse into the possibility of powerful female rulers in Celtic societies.

The existence of a historical Medb further supports the notion that women in Celtic societies held positions of power and authority. It challenges the patriarchal lens through which history has often been written, highlighting the need to reevaluate and uncover the hidden histories of women in Celtic cultures.

3.2.5 Medb's Legacy and Influence

Medb's legacy extends beyond the realm of mythology and history. Her character continues to inspire and captivate audiences, serving as a symbol of female empowerment and resilience. Medb's story resonates with modern readers, reminding them of the strength and capabilities of women throughout history.

Furthermore, Medb's role in Táin Bó Cúailnge and her representation in Celtic mythology contribute to the ongoing discussions surrounding gender fluidity in Celtic cultures. The acceptance and recognition of powerful female figures like Medb challenge traditional gender norms and highlight the cultural significance of gender fluidity in Celtic societies.

By examining Medb's role in Táin Bó Cúailnge, we gain a deeper understanding of the complex and multifaceted nature of Celtic societies. Medb's character serves as a testament to the important roles that women played in warfare and leadership, challenging the patriarchal biases that have often overshadowed their contributions. Her story encourages us to reevaluate our understanding of history and archaeology, unveiling the hidden histories of warrior women and their cultural significance.

3.3 Medb as a Symbol of Female Power and Authority

In the realm of Irish mythology, Queen Medb, also known as Maeve, stands as a powerful symbol of female power and authority. Medb's story and her role in the epic tale of Táin

Bó Cúailnge (The Cattle Raid of Cooley) shed light on the significant position women held in Celtic societies. Through her portrayal, we can uncover the hidden histories of Celtic women and challenge the patriarchal biases that have often overshadowed their contributions.

Medb's Role in Táin Bó Cúailnge (The Cattle Raid of Cooley)

Táin Bó Cúailnge is an ancient Irish epic that tells the story of a cattle raid orchestrated by Queen Medb. In this tale, Medb is depicted as a fierce and ambitious ruler who leads her armies into battle to claim the prized bull of Cooley. Her determination and strategic prowess are evident as she navigates the challenges and obstacles that arise during the raid.

Medb's role in Táin Bó Cúailnge showcases her as a skilled military leader, commanding her forces with confidence and authority. She is not merely a passive observer or a figurehead; she actively participates in the planning and execution of the raid, demonstrating her ability to lead and make crucial decisions. Medb's actions challenge the notion that women were solely confined to domestic roles in Celtic societies and highlight their capacity for leadership and warfare.

Medb as a Symbol of Female Power and Authority

Queen Medb's portrayal in Irish mythology goes beyond her role as a military leader. She embodies the qualities of strength, independence, and assertiveness, challenging the traditional gender roles and expectations of Celtic societies. Medb's character represents a powerful archetype of female authority, inspiring generations of women to embrace their own strength and assertiveness.

Medb's story also highlights the importance of female agency and autonomy. She is depicted as a ruler who takes charge of her own destiny, making decisions that shape the course of her kingdom. Her actions and ambitions are not driven by the influence or guidance of male figures but by her own desires and aspirations. Medb's portrayal as a self-determined leader challenges the patriarchal biases that have often downplayed or ignored the agency of women in Celtic societies.

Unveiling the Historical Medb

While Medb's story is rooted in mythology, it is essential to consider the historical context that may have influenced the development of her character. The ancient Celts had a rich oral tradition, and their myths and legends were often shaped by historical events and societal norms. Although it is challenging to separate fact from fiction, the existence of powerful female figures like Medb suggests that women held positions of authority and influence in Celtic societies.

Archaeological evidence also supports the idea that Celtic women played active roles in warfare. The discovery of female burials with weapons and armor indicates that women were not only present on the battlefield but also actively engaged in combat. These findings challenge the patriarchal lens through which history and archaeology have often been written, high-lighting the need to reevaluate our understanding of Celtic societies and the roles of women within them.

The Cultural Significance of Medb

Medb's story and her representation as a symbol of female power and authority have had a lasting impact on Celtic culture and identity. She has become an emblem of strength and resilience, inspiring countless individuals to embrace their own inner warrior spirit. Medb's legacy serves as a reminder of the significant contributions women have made throughout history, challenging the patriarchal biases that have often overshadowed their achievements.

Furthermore, Medb's story emphasizes the importance of gender fluidity in Celtic cultures. The acceptance and recognition of diverse gender identities and expressions were integral to Celtic societies. The existence of warrior women like Medb and the reverence for female figures associated with war and battle, such as the Morrígan, demonstrate the fluidity and complexity of gender roles in Celtic mythology and society.

By exploring Medb's role as a symbol of female power and authority, we can begin to unravel the hidden histories of Celtic women and challenge the patriarchal biases that have shaped our understanding of the past. Medb's story serves as a testament to the strength and resilience of Celtic women, inspiring us to recognize and celebrate their contributions to history and culture.

3.4 Unveiling the Historical Medb

Queen Medb, also known as Maeve, is a prominent figure in Irish mythology and a symbol of female power and authority. While Medb's portrayal in mythology is well-known, there is a need to uncover the historical Medb and explore her significance in Celtic societies. By examining historical sources and archaeological evidence, we can gain a deeper understanding of Medb's role and the impact she had on Celtic women.

3.4.1 Historical Accounts of Queen Medb

Historical accounts of Queen Medb are scarce, as much of what we know about her comes from mythological tales and sagas. However, there are references to a powerful queen named Medb in early Irish literature, suggesting that she may have been a real historical figure. These references describe her as a formidable ruler and a skilled warrior, leading her armies into battle.

One of the most significant sources of information about Medb is the epic tale known as Táin Bó Cúailnge, or The Cattle Raid of Cooley. This tale recounts Medb's quest to obtain the prized bull of Cooley and her role as a military leader during the conflict. While the events of the Táin Bó Cúailnge are steeped in mythology, they provide valuable insights into Medb's character and her position of authority.

3.4.2 Medb's Role in Táin Bó Cúailnge (The Cattle Raid of Cooley)

In the Táin Bó Cúailnge, Medb is depicted as a fierce and determined leader who commands an army of warriors. She is portrayed as a skilled strategist, making tactical decisions and leading her troops into battle. Medb's role in the epic highlights her military prowess and her ability to inspire loyalty and obedience among her followers.

Furthermore, Medb's actions in the Táin Bó Cúailnge challenge traditional gender roles and expectations. She is depicted as a strong and assertive ruler, unafraid to assert her authority and pursue her goals. Medb's character defies the patriarchal norms of her time, showcasing the potential for women to hold positions of power and influence in Celtic societies.

3.4.3 Medb as a Symbol of Female Power and Authority

Medb's portrayal in Irish mythology has made her a symbol of female power and authority. She represents a strong and independent woman who is not afraid to challenge societal norms and assert her own agency. Medb's character resonates with modern audiences, inspiring women to embrace their own strength and leadership potential.

The significance of Medb extends beyond her role as a warrior queen. She embodies the idea that women in Celtic societies had the ability to shape their own destinies and play active roles in political and military affairs. Medb's story challenges the notion that women were solely confined to domestic roles and highlights the complex and multifaceted nature of gender dynamics in Celtic societies.

3.4.4 Unveiling the Historical Medb

Unveiling the historical Medb is a challenging task due to the limited historical sources available. However, by examining the context in which Medb's character emerged and the cultural significance attributed to her, we can gain valuable insights into the role of women in Celtic societies.

While the historical Medb may never be fully revealed, it is important to recognize the impact of her mythological representation. Medb's character serves as a reminder of the potential

for women to hold positions of power and authority in Celtic
societies. Her story challenges the patriarchal biases that have
often downplayed or ignored the contributions of women in
history.

By acknowledging the historical Medb and the significance
of her mythological portrayal, we can begin to unravel the
hidden histories of Celtic women. This exploration allows us
to challenge the patriarchal lens through which history and
archaeology have often been written, and to recognize the
diverse roles and contributions of women in Celtic societies.

Unveiling the historical Medb is not only a scholarly endeavor
but also a means of empowering women today. By uncovering
the stories of powerful women like Medb, we can inspire and
encourage modern women to embrace their own strength, leadership, and agency. The historical Medb serves as a symbol of
resilience and determination, reminding us of the rich cultural
heritage and the potential for gender equality within Celtic
societies.

In the next chapter, we will delve deeper into the female
figures in Celtic mythology, exploring the symbolism and
significance of the Morrígan and other warrior goddesses.
Through this exploration, we will further uncover the complex
and multifaceted roles of women in Celtic cultures.

4

Chapter 4

Female Figures in Celtic Mythology

4.1 The Morrígan

In Celtic mythology, there are several female figures associated with war and battle, and one of the most prominent among them is the Morrígan. The Morrígan is a complex and multifaceted goddess who embodies the power and ferocity of war. She is often depicted as a shape-shifter, taking the form of a crow or raven, and is known for her ability to foretell the outcome of battles.

The Morrígan is often portrayed as a fierce and formidable warrior, inspiring fear and awe in those who encounter her. She is said to have the ability to manipulate the outcome of battles, either by aiding those she favors or by bringing about the downfall of her enemies. In some stories, she is even described as actively participating in the fighting, wielding a spear or a sword with deadly skill.

One of the most well-known tales involving the Morrígan

is the Táin Bó Cúailnge (The Cattle Raid of Cooley), an epic saga from Irish mythology. In this story, the Morrígan plays a significant role in the conflict between the Ulstermen and the Connachtmen, using her powers to influence the outcome of the battle. She appears to the hero Cú Chulainn in various forms, testing his courage and challenging him to prove his worth as a warrior.

The Morrígan's association with war and battle extends beyond her role as a warrior goddess. She is also closely linked to sovereignty and the land, symbolizing the power and authority of the ruling class. In some stories, she is depicted as a queen or a goddess who bestows kingship upon those she deems worthy. This connection between war, sovereignty, and female power challenges the traditional patriarchal narrative that positions men as the sole wielders of authority and military prowess.

While the Morrígan is perhaps the most well-known female figure associated with war in Celtic mythology, she is not the only one. Other warrior goddesses, such as Macha and Badb, also feature prominently in Celtic tales. These goddesses, like the Morrígan, embody the strength and ferocity of battle, challenging the notion that warfare is solely the domain of men.

The presence of these powerful female figures in Celtic mythology suggests that women held a significant role in the cultural imagination of the Celts when it came to warfare. Their inclusion in mythological tales highlights the recognition of women's potential for leadership, combat skills, and strategic thinking.

It is important to note that the stories and myths surrounding the Morrígan and other warrior goddesses in Celtic mythology are not just fictional tales. They reflect the values, beliefs, and social dynamics of the Celtic societies in which they originated.

These myths provide valuable insights into the cultural significance of women's roles in warfare and challenge the patriarchal biases that have often downplayed or ignored the contributions of women in Celtic societies.

The representation of powerful female figures in Celtic mythology also aligns with the archaeological evidence that suggests women did participate in warfare and held positions of authority in some cases. Burial sites have been discovered that contain the remains of women buried with weapons and armor, indicating their involvement in combat. Additionally, ancient texts and historical accounts mention female warriors and leaders, further supporting the idea that women played active roles in Celtic warfare.

The existence of female warriors in Celtic societies challenges the traditional gender roles and expectations that have been imposed by patriarchal societies throughout history. It demonstrates that gender fluidity and the acceptance of diverse gender roles were present in Celtic cultures. This acceptance of gender fluidity allowed women to participate in traditionally male-dominated spheres, such as warfare, and hold positions of power and authority.

The cultural significance of the Morrígan and other female figures in Celtic mythology extends beyond their association with war and battle. They serve as symbols of female empowerment, challenging societal norms and expectations. Their stories inspire and empower modern readers, particularly women, to embrace their own strength, courage, and leadership potential.

By exploring the stories and representations of the Morrígan and other female figures in Celtic mythology, we can gain a deeper understanding of the diverse roles and contributions of women in Celtic societies. These stories provide a counter-narrative to the patriarchal lens through which history and archaeology have often been written, shedding light on the hidden histories of warrior women and their impact on Celtic cultures.

In the following sections, we will delve further into the stories and symbolism of other female figures in Celtic mythology, as well as examine the historical accounts and archaeological evidence of women warriors in Celtic societies. Through this exploration, we hope to challenge stereotypes and misconceptions, and uncover the rich and complex history of warrior women in the Celts.

4.2 Other Warrior Goddesses in Celtic Mythology

In addition to the Morrígan, Celtic mythology is rich with other powerful and fierce warrior goddesses who played significant roles in the ancient Celtic pantheon. These goddesses embody the strength, courage, and skill that were highly valued in Celtic societies. Their stories and symbolism provide further evidence of the important role that women played in Celtic mythology and the potential influence they had in shaping societal norms.

4.2.1 Macha: The Sovereignty Goddess

Macha is a prominent figure in Irish mythology and is often associated with sovereignty, fertility, and war. She is depicted as a powerful goddess who possesses both physical and magical abilities. Macha's story is intertwined with the Ulster Cycle, a collection of tales that revolve around the heroes of Ulster.

One of the most well-known stories involving Macha is the "Cattle Raid of Cooley," where she plays a crucial role. In this tale, Macha challenges the men of Ulster to a race while heavily pregnant. Despite her condition, she outpaces the men and gives birth to twins at the finish line. This feat demonstrates her physical strength and endurance, as well as her ability to defy societal expectations.

Macha's association with war is evident in her role as a sovereignty goddess. In Celtic mythology, the sovereignty goddess represents the land and its prosperity. The king must marry the goddess to ensure the fertility and well-being of the kingdom. Macha's connection to war suggests that women had a significant influence on the outcome of battles and the success of their communities.

4.2.2 Rhiannon: The Divine Queen

Rhiannon is a Welsh goddess who is often depicted as a queen and a horse goddess. She is associated with sovereignty, fertility, and the Otherworld. Rhiannon's story is told in the Mabinogion, a collection of Welsh myths and legends.

One of the most famous tales involving Rhiannon is the story of "Pwyll, Prince of Dyfed." In this story, Rhiannon is pursued by suitors who desire her hand in marriage. However, she rejects them and chooses Pwyll, a mortal prince, as her husband. Rhiannon's agency in choosing her own partner highlights her autonomy and power as a woman.

Rhiannon's association with horses is significant as well. Horses were highly valued in Celtic societies for their speed and strength in battle. As a horse goddess, Rhiannon embodies these qualities and may have been revered as a protector and guide for warriors.

4.2.3 Epona: The Horse Goddess

Epona is a Gaulish goddess who is widely worshipped through-out the Celtic world. She is primarily associated with horses, fertility, and abundance. Epona is often depicted riding a horse or surrounded by horses, emphasizing her connection to these animals.

As a horse goddess, Epona played a vital role in Celtic society. Horses were not only used for transportation and agriculture but also played a significant role in warfare. The Celts were skilled horse riders and utilized cavalry in battle. Epona's association with horses suggests that she may have been revered as a protector and patroness of warriors.

Epona's depiction as a goddess of fertility and abundance also highlights the importance of women in Celtic society. Fertility was highly valued, and women played a crucial role in ensuring the prosperity and continuation of their communities. Epona's presence in Celtic mythology reinforces the idea that women held positions of power and influence.

4.2.4 Scáthach: The Warrior Queen

Scáthach is a legendary warrior queen in Irish mythology. She is renowned for her skill in combat and is often depicted as a teacher of warriors. Scáthach's story is closely associated with the hero Cú Chulainn, whom she trains in the art of war.

Scáthach's role as a warrior queen challenges traditional gender roles and highlights the importance of women in warfare. She is depicted as a formidable and respected leader, command-ing her own army and imparting her knowledge and skills to aspiring warriors. Scáthach's presence in Celtic mythology suggests that women not only participated in warfare but also held positions of authority and expertise.

4.2.5 Other Warrior Women in Celtic Mythology

In addition to the goddesses mentioned above, there are several other female figures in Celtic mythology who are associated with war and battle. These include Aife, a warrior queen and rival of Scáthach, and Deirdre, a tragic heroine who possesses beauty and courage.

The presence of these warrior goddesses and female figures in Celtic mythology provides further evidence of the significant roles that women played in Celtic societies. Their stories challenge the patriarchal biases that have often downplayed or ignored the contributions of women in history and mythology.

By exploring the tales and symbolism of these warrior goddesses, we can gain a deeper understanding of the cultural significance of women in Celtic societies. These myths and legends serve as a reminder of the strength, courage, and agency that women possessed, and their potential influence in shaping societal norms.

The next chapter will delve into the stories of female heroes and warriors in Celtic mythological tales, further highlighting the diverse roles and contributions of women in Celtic societies.

4.3 Female Heroes and Warriors in Mythological Tales

In addition to the historical accounts of warrior women in Celtic societies, there is also a rich tradition of female heroes and warriors in Celtic mythology. These mythological tales provide further evidence of the significant role that women played in

Celtic cultures, challenging the patriarchal biases that have often overshadowed their contributions. By exploring these mythological figures, we can gain a deeper understanding of the cultural significance and symbolism associated with Celtic female warriors.

4.3.1 The Morrígan: Goddess of War and Battle

One of the most prominent and powerful female figures in Celtic mythology is the Morrígan, the goddess of war and battle. She is often depicted as a shape-shifter, capable of transforming into various forms, including a crow or raven. The Morrígan is associated with sovereignty, prophecy, and the protection of the land. She is known to appear on the battlefield, inspiring warriors and determining the outcome of conflicts.

In mythological tales, the Morrígan is often portrayed as an active participant in battles, engaging in combat alongside male warriors. She is said to have the ability to shape the outcome of a battle through her presence and influence. This portrayal of the Morrígan as a warrior goddess highlights the importance of female power and agency in Celtic mythology.

4.3.2 Other Warrior Goddesses in Celtic Mythology

In addition to the Morrígan, there are several other warrior goddesses in Celtic mythology who embody strength, courage, and martial prowess. One such figure is Macha, who is associated with sovereignty and the protection of the land. In the mythological tale of the Ulster Cycle, Macha challenges the men of Ulster to a race while heavily pregnant and emerges victorious, demonstrating her physical and mental fortitude.

Another notable warrior goddess is Badb, who is often depicted as a crow or raven and is associated with battle and prophecy. She is known to appear on the battlefield, inspiring fear and confusion among the enemy. Badb's presence signifies the imminent arrival of conflict and serves as a reminder of the power and influence of female warriors in Celtic mythology.

4.3.3 Female Heroes and Warriors in Mythological Tales

Beyond the realm of goddesses, Celtic mythology also features several female heroes and warriors who play significant roles in mythological tales. These figures challenge traditional gender roles and highlight the agency and strength of women in Celtic cultures.

One such example is Scáthach, a legendary warrior woman and teacher of martial arts. Scáthach is known for her exceptional combat skills and is said to have trained the hero Cú Chulainn in the art of war. Her portrayal as a skilled warrior and mentor demonstrates the recognition and respect given to women in positions of authority and expertise.

Another notable female warrior is Étain, who is associated with beauty, love, and transformation. In the mythological tale of "The Wooing of Étain," she is depicted as a powerful and independent woman who defies societal expectations and chooses her own path. Étain's story challenges the notion that women in Celtic societies were solely confined to domestic roles and highlights their ability to shape their own destinies.

4.3.4 Exploring the Symbolism of Celtic Female Figures

The presence of female heroes and warriors in Celtic mythology serves as a powerful symbol of female strength, agency, and resilience. These figures embody qualities traditionally associated with masculinity, challenging the notion that women are inherently weaker or less capable in the realm of warfare.

The symbolism associated with Celtic female figures extends beyond the battlefield. They represent the interconnectedness of power, sovereignty, and the natural world. These mythological tales emphasize the importance of balance and harmony between genders, recognizing the unique contributions and strengths that both men and women bring to society.

By exploring the stories of these female figures in Celtic mythology, we can gain a deeper appreciation for the cultural significance of women's roles in Celtic societies. These tales challenge the patriarchal biases that have often downplayed or ignored the different roles of women in history and archaeology. They provide a powerful reminder of the importance of recognizing and celebrating the diverse contributions of women throughout history.

In the next chapter, we will delve into the historical accounts of women warriors in Celtic societies, further solidifying the evidence of their participation in warfare and positions of power. We will examine the archaeological findings and explore the societal implications of these discoveries. Through this exploration, we will continue to challenge stereotypes and misconceptions, shedding light on the rich and complex history of Celtic warrior women.

4.4 Exploring the Symbolism of Celtic Female Figures

Throughout Celtic mythology, there are numerous female figures who are associated with war, battle, and strength. These powerful women serve as symbols of courage, resilience, and the indomitable spirit of the Celtic people. By delving into the symbolism of these female figures, we can gain a deeper understanding of the cultural significance they held in Celtic societies.

4.4.1 The Morrígan: Goddess of War and Battle

One of the most prominent and revered female figures in Celtic mythology is the Morrígan, the goddess of war and battle. She is often depicted as a shape-shifter, taking the form of a crow or raven, and is associated with fate, prophecy, and sovereignty. The Morrígan is known for her fierce and relentless nature, embodying the ferocity and determination of Celtic warriors.

In Celtic mythology, the Morrígan frequently appears on the battlefield, inspiring warriors and influencing the outcome of battles. She is often seen as a harbinger of death and destruction, but also as a protector and guardian of the Celtic people. The symbolism of the Morrígan represents the power and strength of women in Celtic societies, challenging the notion that women were solely confined to domestic roles.

4.4.2 Other Warrior Goddesses in Celtic Mythology

In addition to the Morrígan, Celtic mythology is replete with other warrior goddesses who embody the strength and bravery of Celtic women. One such goddess is Macha, who is associated with sovereignty, war, and horses. Macha is known for her role in the Ulster Cycle, where she challenges the male warriors of Ulster to a race while heavily pregnant, ultimately winning and cursing the men with a debilitating pain during times of crisis.

Another notable warrior goddess is Badb, who is often depicted as a crow or raven and is associated with battle, prophecy, and sovereignty. Badb is known for her ability to shape-shift and her role in inspiring warriors on the battlefield. She is a symbol of the destructive power of war and the importance of female agency in Celtic societies.

4.4.3 Female Heroes and Warriors in Mythological Tales

Celtic mythology also features numerous tales of female heroes and warriors who defy societal expectations and demonstrate their prowess in battle. These stories challenge the patriarchal biases that have often downplayed or ignored the roles of women in Celtic societies.

One such example is Scáthach, a legendary warrior woman and teacher of the hero Cú Chulainn. Scáthach is renowned for her skill in combat and her ability to train warriors. Her inclusion in mythological tales highlights the recognition and respect given to women warriors in Celtic societies.

Another notable figure is Étain, a princess who becomes a warrior and plays a crucial role in the Táin Bó Cúailnge (The Cattle Raid of Cooley). Étain's bravery and skill in battle demonstrate the agency and capabilities of Celtic women, challenging the notion that they were solely confined to domestic roles.

4.4.4 Exploring the Symbolism

The symbolism of Celtic female figures in mythology goes beyond their association with war and battle. These figures represent the strength, resilience, and agency of women in Celtic societies. They challenge the patriarchal lens through which history and archaeology have often been written, shedding light on the diverse roles and contributions of women.

The symbolism of these female figures also highlights the cultural significance of gender fluidity in Celtic societies. The ability of the Morrígan and other goddesses to shape-shift represents the fluidity of gender roles and the recognition of the power and strength that can be found in both masculine and feminine qualities.

By exploring the symbolism of Celtic female figures, we can gain a deeper appreciation for the rich and complex history of women in Celtic societies. These figures serve as powerful reminders of the important roles women played in warfare, leadership, and shaping the cultural fabric of Celtic communities.

As we continue to challenge patriarchal biases and unveil hidden histories, it is crucial to recognize the contributions of Celtic women and the importance of gender fluidity in understanding their roles. By embracing the lessons from Celtic cultures, we can strive for a more inclusive and equitable society that values and celebrates the diverse contributions of all genders.

5

Chapter 5

Women Warriors in Celtic History

5.1 Historical Accounts of Women Warriors

Throughout history, the role of women in warfare has often been overlooked or downplayed. However, in Celtic societies, there is evidence to suggest that women not only participated in warfare but also held positions of power and authority. By examining historical accounts, we can shed light on the significant contributions of women warriors in Celtic history.

5.1.1 Celtic Women in Battle

Historical accounts provide glimpses into the lives of Celtic women warriors who defied societal norms and actively participated in battles. One such prominent figure is Boudica, also known as Boadicea, the warrior queen of the Iceni tribe in Britain. Boudica led a rebellion against the Roman Empire in 60–61 CE, displaying exceptional military leadership and strategic prowess. Her fierce determination and bravery inspired her people to rise up against their oppressors.

Another notable example is Queen Medb, also known as Maeve, from Irish mythology. While her existence as a historical figure is debated, Medb is depicted as a powerful and formidable queen who led her armies into battle. In the epic tale of Táin Bó Cúailnge (The Cattle Raid of Cooley), Medb's military prowess and leadership skills are highlighted as she leads her forces against the Ulaidh.

5.1.2 Archaeological Evidence

Archaeological discoveries further support the existence of women warriors in Celtic societies. Excavations have unearthed grave sites containing weapons and armor traditionally associated with warfare, alongside female remains. These findings challenge the notion that women were solely confined to domestic roles and provide tangible evidence of their active participation in battle.

For instance, the discovery of the "Warrior of Hirschlanden" in Germany revealed a burial site containing the remains of a woman buried with a sword and other military equipment. This finding suggests that women not only fought alongside men but also held high-ranking positions within Celtic armies.

5.1.3 Literary and Mythological Accounts

Celtic mythology is replete with powerful female figures associated with war and battle. The Morrígan, a goddess of war and sovereignty, is one such example. She is often depicted as a shape-shifter who appears on the battlefield, inspiring warriors and foretelling the outcome of battles. The Morrígan's presence in Celtic mythology highlights the cultural significance of women's involvement in warfare.

Other female figures in Celtic mythology, such as Scáthach and Aife, are renowned warrior queens who trained heroes in the art of combat. These mythological accounts not only reflect the cultural acceptance of women warriors but also emphasize their importance and influence in Celtic societies.

5.1.4 Historical Context and Interpretation

It is important to consider the historical context and the lens through which history has been written when examining the role of women warriors in Celtic societies. The patriarchal biases prevalent in historical and archaeological research have often marginalized or ignored the contributions of women. As a result, the true extent of women's involvement in warfare may have been underestimated.

However, by reevaluating existing evidence and challenging traditional interpretations, scholars are beginning to uncover the hidden histories of women warriors. This reexamination allows us to appreciate the diverse roles women played in Celtic societies and the impact they had on their communities.

5.1.5 Challenging Stereotypes and Misconceptions

The existence of women warriors in Celtic societies challenges the stereotypes and misconceptions surrounding gender roles in ancient civilizations. It demonstrates that women were not passive bystanders but active participants in shaping their societies. By acknowledging and celebrating the contributions of women warriors, we can challenge the patriarchal biases that have influenced historical narratives.

Furthermore, the recognition of women warriors in Celtic history highlights the importance of gender fluidity in Celtic cultures. Celtic societies embraced a more fluid understanding of gender, allowing individuals to transcend traditional gender roles. This acceptance of gender fluidity allowed women to assume positions of power and authority, including in warfare.

In conclusion, historical accounts, archaeological evidence, and mythological tales all point to the existence of women warriors in Celtic societies. These women defied societal norms, actively participated in battles, and held positions of power and authority. By challenging stereotypes and acknowledging the importance of gender fluidity, we can unveil the hidden histories of women warriors and appreciate their significant contributions to Celtic cultures.

5.2 Evidence of Women's Participation in Warfare

The participation of women in warfare is a topic that has been widely debated and often overlooked in historical narratives. However, when examining Celtic societies, there is compelling evidence to suggest that women not only participated in warfare but also held positions of power and authority. This evidence challenges the patriarchal biases that have shaped our under-standing of Celtic history and highlights the importance of unveiling hidden histories.

5.2.1 Burial Sites and Grave Goods

One of the most significant pieces of evidence for women's participation in warfare comes from the examination of burial sites and grave goods. Archaeological excavations have revealed the presence of weapons, armor, and other military equipment in the graves of Celtic women. These findings indicate that women were not only involved in warfare but also held high-ranking positions within their communities.

For example, the burial site of a Celtic woman discovered in Hochdorf, Germany, contained a rich array of grave goods, including a sword, shield, and chariot. These items suggest that she held a prominent role in her society and may have been a warrior or a leader. Similar findings have been made in other Celtic burial sites, further supporting the notion that women played active roles in warfare.

5.2.2 Historical Accounts and Chronicles

Historical accounts and chronicles from ancient sources also provide evidence of women's participation in warfare. One of the most well-known examples is the warrior queen Boudica (Boadicea), who led a rebellion against the Roman Empire in 60-61 CE. Boudica's military campaigns and her ability to rally her people demonstrate her leadership skills and her role as a warrior.

Another prominent figure is Queen Medb (Maeve) from Irish mythology. While her existence as a historical figure is debated, the mythological accounts depict her as a powerful and formidable queen who led her armies into battle. The Táin Bó Cúailnge (The Cattle Raid of Cooley) is a tale that highlights

Medb's military prowess and her role as a warrior queen.

5.2.3 Artistic Representations

Artistic representations, such as carvings and statues, also provide insights into the participation of women in warfare. The Morrígan, a goddess associated with war and battle in Celtic mythology, is often depicted as a fierce warrior. She is shown wielding weapons and wearing armor, emphasizing her role as a powerful figure in Celtic society.

Other female figures in Celtic mythology, such as Scáthach and Aife, are also portrayed as skilled warriors and trainers of heroes. These depictions suggest that women were not only involved in warfare but also held positions of authority as teachers and leaders in combat.

5.2.4 Historical and Legal Texts

Historical and legal texts from Celtic societies also offer glimpses into the roles of women in warfare. The Brehon Laws, a legal system used in ancient Ireland, mention the rights and responsibilities of women in relation to warfare. These laws acknowledge the participation of women in battle and outline their entitlement to compensation and protection.

Additionally, the writings of ancient Greek and Roman historians, such as Julius Caesar and Tacitus, mention the presence of Celtic women in warfare. Caesar, in his account of the Gallic Wars, describes Celtic women fighting alongside men and displaying great courage and skill in battle.

5.2.5 Oral Traditions and Folklore

Oral traditions and folklore provide another layer of evidence for women's participation in warfare. Celtic societies had a rich tradition of storytelling, and many tales and legends feature female warriors and heroines. These stories, passed down through generations, reflect the cultural significance of women's roles in warfare and their contributions to Celtic society.

The existence of these various forms of evidence challenges the patriarchal lens through which history and archaeology have often been written. It highlights the need to reevaluate our understanding of Celtic societies and recognize the diverse roles that women played. By acknowledging the evidence of women's participation in warfare, we can uncover hidden histories and give voice to the warrior women of the Celts.

The importance of gender fluidity in Celtic cultures cannot be overlooked. Celtic societies had a more fluid understanding of gender roles, allowing for greater flexibility and acceptance of diverse gender identities. This acceptance is evident in the mythological tales that feature gender-shifting deities and heroes. The Morrígan, for example, is often depicted as shifting between the forms of a woman, a crow, and a wolf.

The cultural significance of gender fluidity in Celtic societies extends beyond mythology. It challenges the binary understanding of gender and emphasizes the importance of embracing and celebrating diversity. By exploring the gender fluidity present in Celtic cultures, we can learn valuable lessons about acceptance, equality, and the empowerment of all individuals.

In conclusion, the evidence of women's participation in warfare in Celtic societies is compelling and multifaceted. Burial sites, historical accounts, artistic representations, legal texts, and oral traditions all contribute to our understanding of the roles and contributions of women in Celtic warfare. By recognizing and celebrating the warrior women of the Celts, we can challenge patriarchal biases, unveil hidden histories, and inspire future generations to embrace gender equality and fluidity.

5.3 Women in Celtic Armies and Battle Strategies

Throughout history, women have often been overlooked or marginalized in narratives of warfare and military strategy. However, evidence from Celtic societies suggests that women played active roles in their armies and contributed to battle strategies. By examining historical accounts and archaeological findings, we can begin to uncover the hidden stories of these warrior women and challenge the patriarchal biases that have shaped our understanding of Celtic societies.

5.3.1 Women Warriors in Celtic Armies

Historical accounts provide glimpses of women warriors in Celtic armies, defying traditional gender roles and actively participating in warfare. The writings of ancient Roman historians such as Tacitus and Dio Cassius mention the presence of Celtic women on the battlefield. They describe Celtic women fighting alongside men, displaying remarkable bravery and skill in combat.

One notable example is Boudica, the warrior queen who led a rebellion against the Roman Empire in 60-61 CE. Boudica's leadership and military campaigns demonstrated her prowess as a warrior and her ability to command an army. Her actions challenged the prevailing gender norms of the time and showcased the strength and courage of Celtic women in battle.

5.3.2 Battle Strategies and Tactics

The participation of women in Celtic armies also extended to their involvement in battle strategies and tactics. Celtic societies valued the contributions of women in warfare and recognized their strategic acumen. Women played crucial roles in planning and organizing military campaigns, offering their insights and expertise to ensure the success of their armies.

In Celtic mythology, the Morrígan, the goddess of war and battle, is often depicted as a figure who guides and advises warriors in their military endeavors. This portrayal suggests that women in Celtic societies were not only skilled fighters but also possessed a deep understanding of battle strategies and tactics.

Archaeological evidence further supports the notion of women's involvement in battle strategies. The discovery of weapons and armor in female burials indicates that women were equipped for combat and actively participated in military affairs. These findings challenge the traditional narrative that women were solely responsible for domestic and nurturing roles within Celtic societies.

5.3.3 Women's Roles in Celtic Battle

The roles of women in Celtic armies were diverse and multifaceted. While some women fought alongside men on the front lines, others played crucial support roles behind the scenes.

Women served as healers, tending to the wounded and providing medical assistance during and after battles. They also acted as spiritual guides, offering prayers and rituals to protect and empower their warriors.

Celtic women's participation in battle was not limited to a single social class or age group. Women from various backgrounds, including noblewomen and commoners, took up arms and fought for their communities. This inclusivity highlights the egalitarian nature of Celtic societies and challenges the notion that warfare was exclusively a male domain.

5.3.4 Challenging Stereotypes and Misconceptions

The existence of women warriors in Celtic societies challenges long-held stereotypes and misconceptions about gender roles in ancient civilizations. The patriarchal lens through which history and archaeology have often been written has downplayed or ignored the different roles of women in Celtic societies. By uncovering the stories of these warrior women, we can begin to dismantle these biases and present a more accurate and inclusive narrative of Celtic history.

Understanding the contributions of women in Celtic armies not only provides a more comprehensive view of the past but also has important implications for modern society. It challenges the notion that women are inherently weaker or less capable in combat and highlights the importance of gender equality in all aspects of life.

Conclusion

The evidence from historical accounts, archaeological findings, and mythology suggests that women in Celtic societies actively participated in warfare and held positions of authority within their armies. Their involvement in battle strategies and tactics, as well as their diverse roles on the battlefield, challenge traditional gender norms and highlight the strength and resilience of Celtic women.

By recognizing and celebrating the contributions of these warrior women, we can reshape our understanding of Celtic societies and inspire a more inclusive and equitable future. The importance of gender fluidity in Celtic cultures further emphasizes the cultural significance of women's roles and challenges the rigid gender binaries that have often limited women's opportunities throughout history. As we continue to explore and uncover the hidden histories of Celtic warrior women, we must strive to create a society that values and empowers women in all spheres of life.

5.4 Challenging Stereotypes and Misconceptions

Throughout history, the roles and contributions of women in Celtic societies have often been overlooked or downplayed due to the patriarchal lens through which history and archaeology have been written. However, there is a growing body of evidence that challenges these stereotypes and misconceptions, revealing that Celtic women did participate in warfare and held positions of power in some cases. By examining the historical accounts, archaeological findings, and mythological tales, we can begin to unveil the hidden histories of warrior women in Celtic societies.

5.4.1 Reevaluating Historical Accounts

When we delve into the historical accounts of Celtic societies, we find glimpses of women warriors who defied societal norms and played active roles in warfare. One such prominent figure is Boudica, also known as Boadicea, the warrior queen who led a rebellion against the Roman Empire in 60-61 CE. Boudica's military campaigns and leadership skills demonstrate that women were not only capable of participating in warfare but also excelling in it. Her legacy serves as a testament to the strength and resilience of Celtic women.

Another figure worth exploring is Queen Medb, also known as Maeve, from Irish mythology. While her existence as a historical figure is debated, the mythological accounts depict her as a powerful and authoritative queen who led her armies into battle. Medb's role in the epic tale of Táin Bó Cúailnge (The Cattle Raid of Cooley) showcases her strategic prowess and determination. Although her portrayal may be rooted in mythology, it reflects the cultural significance of female power and authority in Celtic societies.

5.4.2 Unveiling Celtic Mythology

Celtic mythology is rich with female figures associated with war and battle. The Morrígan, the goddess of war and battle, is one such prominent example. She is often depicted as a shape-shifter who appears on the battlefield, inspiring warriors and foretelling the outcome of battles. The Morrígan's presence in Celtic mythology highlights the cultural significance of female warriors and their connection to the divine.

Other warrior goddesses, such as Macha and Badb, also

feature prominently in Celtic mythology. These goddesses embody the strength, courage, and ferocity often associated with warriors. Their inclusion in mythological tales suggests that the concept of women as warriors was not only accepted but celebrated in Celtic cultures.

Furthermore, Celtic mythology is replete with stories of female heroes and warriors who display exceptional bravery and skill in battle. Characters like Scáthach, a warrior queen who trained the legendary hero Cú Chulainn, and Aife, a warrior woman who challenged Cú Chulainn in combat, challenge the notion that women were passive participants in Celtic warfare. These tales provide further evidence of the existence and recognition of women warriors in Celtic societies.

5.4.3 Challenging Stereotypes and Misconceptions

The patriarchal lens through which history and archaeology have often been written has perpetuated stereotypes and misconceptions about the roles of women in Celtic societies. However, by reevaluating the available evidence, we can challenge these biases and shed light on the diverse and complex experiences of Celtic women.

Archaeological findings, such as grave goods and weaponry, provide tangible evidence of women's participation in warfare. The discovery of female burials with weapons and armor suggests that women not only fought alongside men but also held positions of authority within Celtic armies. These findings challenge the notion that women were solely confined to domestic roles and highlight the fluidity of gender roles in Celtic societies.

Moreover, the cultural significance of gender fluidity in Celtic cultures cannot be ignored. The existence of warrior women and the acceptance of gender fluidity in mythological tales and historical accounts indicate a more inclusive and nuanced understanding of gender roles. This challenges the binary view of gender that has often been imposed by patriarchal societies.

5.4.4 Lessons for Modern Society

The exploration of warrior women in Celtic societies and the importance of gender fluidity hold valuable lessons for modern society. By recognizing and celebrating the contributions of women in history, we can challenge the patriarchal biases that have shaped our understanding of the past. This recognition can inspire and empower women today, providing them with role models who defied societal expectations and achieved greatness.

Furthermore, the cultural significance of gender fluidity in Celtic societies serves as a reminder that gender is not fixed or limited to a binary construct. Embracing gender fluidity allows for a more inclusive and diverse society, where individuals are free to express their true selves without fear of judgment or discrimination.

In conclusion, the evidence suggests that women in Celtic societies did participate in warfare and held positions of power. By challenging stereotypes and misconceptions, we can unveil the hidden histories of warrior women in Celtic cultures. The importance of gender fluidity in Celtic societies and its cultural significance provide valuable insights for modern society. By recognizing and celebrating the contributions of women and embracing gender fluidity, we can create a more equitable and inclusive world.

6.1 Women's Roles in Celtic Communities

Celtic societies were complex and diverse, with women playing significant roles beyond warfare. While the previous chapters have focused on the warrior women of the Celts, it is important to explore the broader roles and contributions of women in Celtic communities. This chapter aims to shed light on the multifaceted nature of women's roles in Celtic societies, highlighting their involvement in politics, leadership positions, economic activities, and their cultural significance.

6.1.1 Women in Politics and Leadership Positions

Contrary to the prevailing patriarchal biases, Celtic women held positions of power and authority within their communities. Historical accounts and mythological tales provide evidence of women who were influential leaders and rulers. One notable example is Queen Boudica (Boadicea), who not only led her people in battle but also held political power as the queen of the Iceni tribe. Boudica's leadership and her ability to rally her people against the Roman invaders demonstrate the respect and authority she commanded.

In addition to Boudica, Queen Medb (Maeve) from Irish mythology is another example of a powerful female leader. Medb is depicted as a queen who ruled over the Connacht region and was known for her political prowess and military campaigns. Her role in the epic tale of Táin Bó Cúailnge (The Cattle Raid of Cooley) showcases her determination and strategic abilities.

These examples highlight that women in Celtic societies were not confined to domestic roles but actively participated in political affairs and held positions of leadership. Their influence extended beyond the household, challenging the notion that women were solely responsible for the private sphere.

6.1.2 Women's Economic Contributions

Women in Celtic societies were not only active in politics but also made significant economic contributions. They played crucial roles in agriculture, trade, and craftsmanship, contributing to the overall prosperity of their communities. Archaeological evidence reveals the presence of women engaged in farming activities, such as tending to crops and livestock.

Moreover, Celtic women were skilled artisans, creating intricate jewelry, textiles, and pottery. Their craftsmanship was highly valued, and their creations were often traded and exchanged within and beyond Celtic territories. The economic independence and expertise of Celtic women challenge the notion that they were solely dependent on men for their livelihoods.

6.1.3 Cultural Significance of Women's Roles

The roles of women in Celtic societies held cultural significance and were deeply intertwined with their religious and mythological beliefs. Celtic mythology is replete with female figures associated with war and battle, such as the Morrígan, a goddess of war and sovereignty. These mythological representations reflect the cultural recognition of women's power and authority.

Furthermore, the symbolism of Celtic female figures extends beyond warfare. They embody various aspects of life, including fertility, healing, and wisdom. This multifaceted representation emphasizes the diverse roles and capabilities of women in Celtic societies. It challenges the narrow view that women were solely warriors and highlights their integral role in the overall fabric of Celtic culture.

The recognition of women's roles in Celtic communities goes beyond the realm of warfare. It acknowledges their agency, contributions, and influence in various spheres of life. By exploring the broader roles of women, we can gain a more comprehensive understanding of Celtic societies and challenge the patriarchal biases that have often overshadowed their contributions.

In the next chapter, we will delve deeper into the biases present in historical and archaeological research, which have often downplayed or ignored the different roles of women in Celtic societies. By uncovering hidden histories and reevaluating existing narratives, we can gain a more accurate and inclusive understanding of the Celtic past.

6.2 Women in Politics and Leadership Positions

Throughout history, women have often been overlooked or marginalized in discussions of politics and leadership. However, in Celtic societies, there is evidence to suggest that women held positions of power and influence. This chapter will explore the roles of women in politics and leadership positions within Celtic communities, shedding light on their contributions and challenging patriarchal biases.

6.2.1 Political Power and Authority

In Celtic societies, political power was not solely reserved for men. Women played significant roles in governance and decision-making processes. They held positions of authority and were respected for their wisdom and leadership skills. Historical accounts and mythological tales provide glimpses into the political power wielded by Celtic women.

One notable example is Boudica, the warrior queen who led a rebellion against the Roman Empire in the 1st century CE. Boudica not only commanded an army but also held political authority as the leader of the Iceni tribe. Her actions and leadership demonstrated that women could hold positions of power and influence in Celtic society.

6.2.2 Queens and Rulers

Celtic history is replete with examples of powerful queens and rulers who played pivotal roles in shaping their communities. Queen Medb, also known as Maeve, is a prominent figure in Irish mythology. She is depicted as a queen who ruled over the Connacht province and led her people in various battles. Medb's leadership and political prowess highlight the significant role women played in Celtic politics.

Other Celtic societies also had female rulers. The Gauls, for instance, had queens who held political power and were involved in decision-making processes. These queens were not merely figureheads but actively participated in governance and diplomacy, representing their people in negotiations and alliances.

6.2.3 Councils and Assemblies

Celtic societies had councils and assemblies where important decisions were made. Women were not excluded from these gatherings but actively participated and had their voices heard. Historical accounts mention women attending and contributing to these assemblies, offering their insights and opinions on matters of governance and community affairs.

In some cases, women even held positions of authority within these councils. They were respected for their wisdom and were valued as advisors and decision-makers. This demonstrates that women in Celtic societies had the opportunity to shape political discourse and influence the direction of their communities.

6.2.4 Priestesses and Spiritual Leaders

Religion and spirituality held significant importance in Celtic societies, and women played crucial roles as priestesses and spiritual leaders. These positions often carried political influence as well. The Druids, the religious class of the Celts, included both men and women, and female Druids held positions of authority and respect.

The Morrígan, a goddess associated with war and battle, was revered by the Celts. She was often depicted as a powerful figure who could shape the outcome of conflicts. The presence of female deities associated with war suggests that women held esteemed positions in Celtic society, not only in the political realm but also in the spiritual and religious spheres.

6.2.5 Legacy and Impact

The existence of women in politics and leadership positions within Celtic societies challenges the patriarchal biases that have often downplayed or ignored their contributions. Recognizing and acknowledging the roles of women in governance and decision-making processes is crucial for a more accurate understanding of Celtic history.

The cultural significance of women's political power in Celtic societies cannot be overstated. It demonstrates that gender roles were not rigidly defined, and women had agency and influence in shaping their communities. This challenges the notion that women were solely confined to domestic roles and highlights the importance of gender fluidity in Celtic cultures.

By examining the historical and mythological evidence, we can gain a deeper appreciation for the diverse roles women played in Celtic societies. Their political power and leadership positions serve as an inspiration for modern women, reminding us of the strength and capabilities of women throughout history.

In the next chapter, we will explore the economic contributions of women in Celtic societies, shedding light on their roles in trade, craftsmanship, and other economic activities.

6.3 Women's Economic Contributions

Women in Celtic societies played a significant role not only in warfare and leadership positions but also in the economic sphere. While their contributions in this area have often been overlooked or downplayed, evidence suggests that Celtic women were actively involved in various economic activities, contributing to the prosperity and stability of their communities.

6.3.1 Agriculture and Animal Husbandry

One of the primary economic activities in Celtic societies was agriculture, and women played a crucial role in cultivating the land and tending to livestock. They were responsible for planting and harvesting crops, such as grains, vegetables, and fruits. Women also managed the rearing and breeding of animals, including cattle, sheep, and pigs.

Archaeological evidence, such as the discovery of tools associated with farming and animal husbandry in women's graves, indicates their involvement in these activities. Additionally, ancient texts and folklore often mention women's expertise in agricultural practices, highlighting their knowledge and skills in managing the land and ensuring the sustenance of their communities.

6.3.2 Craftsmanship and Artistry

Celtic women were renowned for their craftsmanship and artistry, excelling in various trades and producing intricate and beautiful objects. They were skilled in metalworking, weaving, pottery, and jewelry making. Women would create exquisite jewelry, such as torcs, brooches, and necklaces, using precious metals and gemstones.

The archaeological record provides evidence of women's involvement in these crafts. For example, the discovery of female burials with tools and materials associated with metalworking suggests their active participation in this trade. Additionally, ancient texts and myths often depict women as skilled weavers and seamstresses, creating elaborate textiles and clothing.

6.3.3 Trade and Commerce

Celtic women were not only involved in the production of goods but also played a role in trade and commerce. They participated in local and long-distance trade networks, exchanging goods and resources with neighboring communities and even distant regions. Women would engage in bartering and selling their products, contributing to the economic growth and development of their societies.

Historical accounts and archaeological findings provide evidence of women's involvement in trade. For instance, the discovery of female burials with valuable imported goods suggests their participation in long-distance trade. Additionally, ancient texts mention women as traders and merchants, highlighting their active role in economic transactions.

6.3.4 Financial Management and Entrepreneurship

Celtic women also demonstrated their financial acumen and entrepreneurial skills. They were involved in managing household finances, making economic decisions, and overseeing the distribution of resources. Women would engage in small-scale businesses, such as running taverns, inns, and shops, contributing to the local economy.

Ancient texts and legal documents mention women's involvement in financial matters, including loans, contracts, and property ownership. These sources indicate that women had the authority to make financial decisions and engage in economic activities independently.

6.3.5 Social and Community Contributions

Women's economic contributions extended beyond individual endeavors and had a broader impact on their communities. They actively participated in communal activities, such as communal farming, where resources and labor were shared among community members. Women would contribute their skills and knowledge to these collective efforts, ensuring the well-being and prosperity of the entire community.

Furthermore, women played a vital role in the production and distribution of food and resources during festivals and religious ceremonies. They would prepare feasts, brew beverages, and create offerings, fostering social cohesion and strengthening community bonds.

6.3.6 Women's Economic Empowerment

The economic contributions of Celtic women were not only essential for the survival and prosperity of their communities but also empowered them on an individual level. Women's economic activities provided them with a sense of agency, independence, and social recognition. By actively participating in economic endeavors, women challenged traditional gender roles and societal expectations, asserting their capabilities and contributions.

The economic empowerment of women in Celtic societies had a profound impact on their status and influence. It allowed them to assert their authority, negotiate power dynamics, and challenge patriarchal norms. Women's economic contributions were not only significant in themselves but also paved the way for their participation in other spheres of society, including politics, leadership, and warfare.

In conclusion, Celtic women made substantial economic contributions to their societies, participating in agriculture, craftsmanship, trade, financial management, and communal activities. Their involvement in these economic endeavors not only ensured the prosperity and stability of their communities but also empowered them on an individual level. Recognizing and celebrating women's economic contributions is crucial for understanding the multifaceted roles they played in Celtic societies and challenging patriarchal biases that have often overshadowed their achievements.

6

Chapter 6

Women in Celtic Society

6.1 Women's Roles in Celtic Communities

Celtic societies were complex and diverse, with women playing significant roles beyond warfare. While the previous chapters have focused on the warrior women of the Celts, it is important to explore the broader roles and contributions of women in Celtic communities. This chapter aims to shed light on the multifaceted nature of women's roles in Celtic societies, highlighting their involvement in politics, leadership positions, economic activities, and their cultural significance.

6.1.1 Women in Politics and Leadership Positions

Contrary to the prevailing patriarchal biases, Celtic women held positions of power and authority within their communities. Historical accounts and mythological tales provide evidence of women who were influential leaders and rulers. One notable example is Queen Boudica (Boadicea), who not only led her people in battle but also held political power as the queen of the Iceni tribe. Boudica's leadership and her ability to rally her people against the Roman invaders demonstrate the respect and authority she commanded.

In addition to Boudica, Queen Medb (Maeve) from Irish mythology is another example of a powerful female leader. Medb is depicted as a queen who ruled over the Connacht region and was known for her political prowess and military campaigns. Her role in the epic tale of Táin Bó Cúailnge (The Cattle Raid of Cooley) showcases her determination and strategic abilities.

These examples highlight that women in Celtic societies were not confined to domestic roles but actively participated in political affairs and held positions of leadership. Their influence extended beyond the household, challenging the notion that women were solely responsible for the private sphere.

6.1.2 Women's Economic Contributions

Women in Celtic societies were not only active in politics but also made significant economic contributions. They played crucial roles in agriculture, trade, and craftsmanship, contributing to the overall prosperity of their communities. Archaeological evidence reveals the presence of women engaged in farming activities, such as tending to crops and livestock.

Moreover, Celtic women were skilled artisans, creating intricate jewelry, textiles, and pottery. Their craftsmanship was highly valued, and their creations were often traded and exchanged within and beyond Celtic territories. The economic independence and expertise of Celtic women challenge the notion that they were solely dependent on men for their liveli-hoods.

6.1.3 Cultural Significance of Women's Roles

The roles of women in Celtic societies held cultural significance and were deeply intertwined with their religious and mytho-logical beliefs. Celtic mythology is replete with female figures associated with war and battle, such as the Morrígan, a goddess of war and sovereignty. These mythological representations reflect the cultural recognition of women's power and authority.

Furthermore, the symbolism of Celtic female figures extends beyond warfare. They embody various aspects of life, including fertility, healing, and wisdom. This multifaceted representation emphasizes the diverse roles and capabilities of women in Celtic societies. It challenges the narrow view that women were solely warriors and highlights their integral role in the overall fabric of Celtic culture.

The recognition of women's roles in Celtic communities goes beyond the realm of warfare. It acknowledges their agency, contributions, and influence in various spheres of life. By exploring the broader roles of women, we can gain a more comprehensive understanding of Celtic societies and challenge the patriarchal biases that have often overshadowed their contributions.

In the next chapter, we will delve deeper into the biases present in historical and archaeological research, which have often downplayed or ignored the different roles of women in Celtic societies. By uncovering hidden histories and reeval-uating existing narratives, we can gain a more accurate and inclusive understanding of the Celtic past.

6.2 Women in Politics and Leadership Positions

Throughout history, women have often been overlooked or marginalized in discussions of politics and leadership. However, in Celtic societies, there is evidence to suggest that women held positions of power and influence. This chapter will explore the roles of women in politics and leadership positions within Celtic communities, shedding light on their contributions and challenging patriarchal biases.

6.2.1 Political Power and Authority

In Celtic societies, political power was not solely reserved for men. Women played significant roles in governance and decision-making processes. They held positions of authority and were respected for their wisdom and leadership skills. Historical accounts and mythological tales provide glimpses into the political power wielded by Celtic women.

One notable example is Boudica, the warrior queen who led a rebellion against the Roman Empire in the 1st century CE. Boudica not only commanded an army but also held political authority as the leader of the Iceni tribe. Her actions and leadership demonstrated that women could hold positions of power and influence in Celtic society.

6.2.2 Queens and Rulers

Celtic history is replete with examples of powerful queens and rulers who played pivotal roles in shaping their communities. Queen Medb, also known as Maeve, is a prominent figure in Irish mythology. She is depicted as a queen who ruled over the

Connacht province and led her people in various battles. Medb's leadership and political prowess highlight the significant role women played in Celtic politics.

Other Celtic societies also had female rulers. The Gauls, for instance, had queens who held political power and were involved in decision-making processes. These queens were not merely figureheads but actively participated in governance and diplomacy, representing their people in negotiations and alliances.

6.2.3 Councils and Assemblies

Celtic societies had councils and assemblies where important decisions were made. Women were not excluded from these gatherings but actively participated and had their voices heard. Historical accounts mention women attending and contributing to these assemblies, offering their insights and opinions on matters of governance and community affairs.

In some cases, women even held positions of authority within these councils. They were respected for their wisdom and were valued as advisors and decision-makers. This demonstrates that women in Celtic societies had the opportunity to shape political discourse and influence the direction of their communities.

6.2.4 Priestesses and Spiritual Leaders

Religion and spirituality held significant importance in Celtic societies, and women played crucial roles as priestesses and spiritual leaders. These positions often carried political influence as well. The Druids, the religious class of the Celts, included both men and women, and female Druids held positions of authority and respect.

The Morrígan, a goddess associated with war and battle, was revered by the Celts. She was often depicted as a powerful figure who could shape the outcome of conflicts. The presence of female deities associated with war suggests that women held esteemed positions in Celtic society, not only in the political realm but also in the spiritual and religious spheres.

6.2.5 Legacy and Impact

The existence of women in politics and leadership positions within Celtic societies challenges the patriarchal biases that have often downplayed or ignored their contributions. Recognizing and acknowledging the roles of women in governance and decision-making processes is crucial for a more accurate understanding of Celtic history.

The cultural significance of women's political power in Celtic societies cannot be overstated. It demonstrates that gender roles were not rigidly defined, and women had agency and influence in shaping their communities. This challenges the notion that women were solely confined to domestic roles and highlights the importance of gender fluidity in Celtic cultures.

By examining the historical and mythological evidence, we can gain a deeper appreciation for the diverse roles women played in Celtic societies. Their political power and leadership positions serve as an inspiration for modern women, reminding us of the strength and capabilities of women throughout history.

In the next chapter, we will explore the economic contributions of women in Celtic societies, shedding light on their roles in trade, craftsmanship, and other economic activities.

6.3 Women's Economic Contributions

Women in Celtic societies played a significant role not only in warfare and leadership positions but also in the economic sphere. While their contributions in this area have often been overlooked or downplayed, evidence suggests that Celtic women were actively involved in various economic activities, contributing to the prosperity and stability of their communities.

6.3.1 Agriculture and Animal Husbandry

One of the primary economic activities in Celtic societies was agriculture, and women played a crucial role in cultivating the land and tending to livestock. They were responsible for planting and harvesting crops, such as grains, vegetables, and fruits. Women also managed the rearing and breeding of animals, including cattle, sheep, and pigs.

Archaeological evidence, such as the discovery of tools associated with farming and animal husbandry in women's graves, indicates their involvement in these activities. Additionally, ancient texts and folklore often mention women's expertise in agricultural practices, highlighting their knowledge and skills in managing the land and ensuring the sustenance of their communities.

6.3.2 Craftsmanship and Artistry

Celtic women were renowned for their craftsmanship and artistry, excelling in various trades and producing intricate and beautiful objects. They were skilled in metalworking, weaving, pottery, and jewelry making. Women would create exquisite jewelry, such as torcs, brooches, and necklaces, using precious metals and gemstones.

The archaeological record provides evidence of women's involvement in these crafts. For example, the discovery of female burials with tools and materials associated with metalworking suggests their active participation in this trade. Additionally, ancient texts and myths often depict women as skilled weavers and seamstresses, creating elaborate textiles and clothing.

6.3.3 Trade and Commerce

Celtic women were not only involved in the production of goods but also played a role in trade and commerce. They participated in local and long-distance trade networks, exchanging goods and resources with neighboring communities and even distant regions. Women would engage in bartering and selling their products, contributing to the economic growth and development of their societies.

Historical accounts and archaeological findings provide evidence of women's involvement in trade. For instance, the discovery of female burials with valuable imported goods suggests their participation in long-distance trade. Additionally, ancient texts mention women as traders and merchants, highlighting their active role in economic transactions.

6.3.4 Financial Management and Entrepreneurship

Celtic women also demonstrated their financial acumen and entrepreneurial skills. They were involved in managing household finances, making economic decisions, and overseeing the distribution of resources. Women would engage in small-scale businesses, such as running taverns, inns, and shops, contributing to the local economy.

Ancient texts and legal documents mention women's involvement in financial matters, including loans, contracts, and property ownership. These sources indicate that women had the authority to make financial decisions and engage in economic activities independently.

6.3.5 Social and Community Contributions

Women's economic contributions extended beyond individual endeavors and had a broader impact on their communities. They actively participated in communal activities, such as communal farming, where resources and labor were shared among community members. Women would contribute their skills and knowledge to these collective efforts, ensuring the well-being and prosperity of the entire community.

Furthermore, women played a vital role in the production and distribution of food and resources during festivals and religious ceremonies. They would prepare feasts, brew beverages, and create offerings, fostering social cohesion and strengthening community bonds.

6.3.6 Women's Economic Empowerment

The economic contributions of Celtic women were not only essential for the survival and prosperity of their communities but also empowered them on an individual level. Women's economic activities provided them with a sense of agency, independence, and social recognition. By actively participating in economic endeavors, women challenged traditional gender roles and societal expectations, asserting their capabilities and contributions.

The economic empowerment of women in Celtic societies had a profound impact on their status and influence. It allowed them to assert their authority, negotiate power dynamics, and challenge patriarchal norms. Women's economic contributions were not only significant in themselves but also paved the way for their participation in other spheres of society, including politics, leadership, and warfare.

In conclusion, Celtic women made substantial economic contributions to their societies, participating in agriculture, craftsmanship, trade, financial management, and communal activities. Their involvement in these economic endeavors not only ensured the prosperity and stability of their communities but also empowered them on an individual level. Recognizing and celebrating women's economic contributions is crucial for understanding the multifaceted roles they played in Celtic societies and challenging patriarchal biases that have often overshadowed their achievements.

6.4 Cultural Significance of Women's Roles

Throughout this book, we have explored the remarkable stories of warrior women in Celtic societies, shedding light on their participation in warfare and their positions of power. However, it is important to recognize that the significance of women's roles in Celtic culture extends far beyond the battlefield. In this section, we will delve into the cultural significance of women's roles in Celtic societies, highlighting their contributions to various aspects of community life.

6.4.1 Women as Guardians of Celtic Culture

In Celtic societies, women played a crucial role in preserving and passing down cultural traditions. They were the keepers of oral history, storytelling, and mythological knowledge. Through their roles as mothers, grandmothers, and community leaders, women ensured the transmission of cultural values, beliefs, and practices from one generation to the next. Their influence extended beyond the domestic sphere, as they actively participated in religious rituals and ceremonies, often serving as priestesses and healers.

6.4.2 Women's Influence in Art and Creativity

Artistic expression held great importance in Celtic societies, and women played a significant role in this realm. They were skilled in various forms of artistic expression, including metalwork, weaving, pottery, and jewelry making. Their creations not only showcased their artistic talents but also served as symbols of cultural identity and status. Women's artistic contributions were highly valued and celebrated, reflecting the recognition of their creative abilities within Celtic communities.

6.4.3 Women's Role in Social Cohesion

Women in Celtic societies were instrumental in fostering social cohesion and maintaining community harmony. They acted as mediators, resolving conflicts and disputes within their communities. Their wisdom, empathy, and ability to understand multiple perspectives made them natural peacemakers. Women's roles in promoting social cohesion extended to their involvement in community decision-making processes, where their opinions and insights were highly regarded.

6.4.4 Women's Influence in Education

Education was highly valued in Celtic societies, and women played a vital role in the education of children. They were responsible for teaching essential skills, knowledge, and values to the younger generation. Women's educational influence extended beyond the household, as they often served as mentors and teachers within their communities. Their wisdom and guidance shaped the minds of future leaders, ensuring the continuity of Celtic cultural heritage.

6.4.5 Women's Contributions to Agriculture and Economy

In Celtic societies, women played a significant role in agricultural practices and economic activities. They were actively involved in farming, animal husbandry, and the cultivation of crops. Women's contributions to the agricultural sector were essential for the sustenance of their communities. Additionally, women engaged in trade and commerce, participating in local and regional markets, and contributing to the economic prosperity of Celtic societies.

6.4.6 Women's Influence in Political and Leadership Roles

While the patriarchal lens has often overshadowed women's roles in politics and leadership, there is evidence to suggest that women held positions of authority in Celtic societies. Historical accounts and mythological tales depict women as queens, chieftains, and advisors, actively participating in decision-making processes and governing their communities. Women's leadership roles were not limited to the domestic sphere but extended to the political and social realms, where their wisdom and guidance were highly valued.

6.4.7 Women's Contributions to Warfare Strategies

In addition to their active participation in warfare, Celtic women made significant contributions to the development of battle strategies. Their knowledge of the terrain, understanding of enemy tactics, and strategic thinking played a crucial role in shaping military campaigns. Women's insights and expertise were sought after by Celtic warriors, highlighting their importance in the planning and execution of military operations.

6.4.8 Women as Symbols of Strength and Resilience

The cultural significance of women's roles in Celtic societies can be seen in the symbolism associated with female figures in mythology and folklore. The Morrígan, for example, embodies the power and ferocity of Celtic warrior women. These mythological representations serve as reminders of the strength, resilience, and courage exhibited by women in Celtic societies. They inspire both men and women to embrace their inner warrior spirit and challenge societal norms and expectations.

In conclusion, the cultural significance of women's roles in Celtic societies cannot be overstated. Women were not only warriors but also guardians of culture, influencers of art and creativity, promoters of social cohesion, educators, contributors to the economy, and leaders in various domains.

7

Chapter 7

Unveiling Hidden Histories

7.1 Biases in Historical and Archaeological Research

Historical and archaeological research plays a crucial role in our understanding of the past. However, it is important to acknowledge that these fields have often been influenced by patriarchal biases, which have shaped the narratives and interpretations of Celtic societies. These biases have led to the downplaying or even erasure of the roles and contributions of women in Celtic societies, particularly in the context of warfare and positions of power.

7.1.1 The Male-Centric Lens

Historical and archaeological research has traditionally been conducted through a male-centric lens, focusing primarily on the experiences and achievements of men. This approach has resulted in a skewed representation of Celtic societies, where women's roles and contributions have been marginalized or overlooked. The emphasis on male warriors and leaders has perpetuated the notion that women were passive and confined to domestic roles, neglecting the evidence that suggests otherwise.

7.1.2 Limited Sources and Interpretations

Another challenge in uncovering the hidden histories of Celtic women is the scarcity of primary sources. Written records from the Celtic period are limited, and the majority of surviving texts were written by male authors, further contributing to the male-centric narrative. Additionally, archaeological evidence can be open to interpretation, and biases can influence how artifacts and burial practices are understood and categorized.

7.1.3 Stereotypes and Misconceptions

Stereotypes and misconceptions about gender roles in Celtic societies have also influenced historical and archaeological research. The prevailing assumption that women were solely responsible for domestic tasks and lacked agency in public life has hindered a more nuanced understanding of their roles. This has resulted in the dismissal or misinterpretation of evidence that suggests women's participation in warfare and positions of authority.

7.1.4 Reevaluating the Evidence

In recent years, scholars have begun to challenge these biases and reevaluate the evidence to uncover the hidden histories of Celtic women. By examining alternative sources and adopting a more inclusive approach, researchers have started to unveil the significant roles that women played in Celtic societies. This reevaluation has shed light on the existence of female warriors, leaders, and powerful figures in Celtic mythology and history.

7.1.5 Rediscovering Women's Stories

One way to overcome biases in historical and archaeological research is to actively seek out and amplify women's stories and experiences. By examining alternative sources, such as folklore, oral traditions, and non-traditional archaeological evidence, researchers have been able to uncover the hidden histories of Celtic women. These stories provide valuable insights into the diverse roles and contributions of women in Celtic societies.

7.1.6 Challenging Assumptions

Challenging assumptions and preconceived notions about gender roles in Celtic societies is essential for a more accurate understanding of the past. By questioning the male-centric narratives and examining the evidence with a critical eye, researchers can begin to challenge the biases that have shaped our understanding of Celtic societies. This process allows for a more inclusive and comprehensive interpretation of the roles and contributions of women.

7.1.7 Importance of Gender Fluidity

The importance of gender fluidity in Celtic cultures cannot be understated. Celtic societies had a more fluid understanding of gender, which allowed for greater flexibility in social roles and expectations. This fluidity is evident in Celtic mythology, where female figures such as the Morrígan were associated with war and battle. By embracing the concept of gender fluidity, we can better appreciate the diverse roles and contributions of women in Celtic societies.

7.1.8 Cultural Significance

Unveiling the hidden histories of Celtic women and challenging patriarchal biases has significant cultural significance. By recognizing and celebrating the roles and contributions of women in Celtic societies, we can challenge traditional narratives and promote a more inclusive understanding of history. This recognition not only empowers women today but also provides a more accurate representation of the past, enriching our collective cultural heritage.

In conclusion, biases in historical and archaeological research have often downplayed or ignored the different roles of women in Celtic societies. However, through reevaluating the evidence, challenging assumptions, and embracing the importance of gender fluidity, we can uncover the hidden histories of Celtic women and gain a more comprehensive understanding of their contributions to society. By recognizing and celebrating these contributions, we can create a more inclusive and accurate narrative of Celtic history.

7.2 Rediscovering Women's Stories and Contributions

Throughout history, the stories and contributions of women have often been overshadowed or even erased by patriarchal biases. This is particularly true when it comes to the history and archaeology of Celtic societies. However, recent research and discoveries have shed light on the important roles that women played in Celtic communities, including their participation in warfare and positions of power. By reevaluating artifacts, burial practices, and historical accounts, we can begin to rediscover the hidden histories of Celtic women and challenge the patriarchal lens through which their stories have been told.

7.2.1 Unveiling Women Warriors

One of the most significant aspects of rediscovering women's stories in Celtic societies is the recognition of their participation in warfare. While the prevailing narrative has often portrayed Celtic warriors as exclusively male, evidence suggests that women also took up arms and fought alongside their male counterparts. Archaeological findings, such as weapons buried with women, depictions of female warriors in art, and historical accounts, all point to the existence of women warriors in Celtic societies.

For example, the legendary figure of Boudica, also known as Boadicea, stands as a testament to the courage and leadership of Celtic women in battle. Boudica led a rebellion against the Roman Empire in 60–61 CE, successfully uniting several Celtic tribes and inflicting significant losses on the Roman forces. Her military campaigns challenged the patriarchal norms of her time and inspired generations of Celtic women to assert their power and agency.

7.2.2 Powerful Queens and Leaders

In addition to their roles as warriors, Celtic women also held positions of power and authority. Queen Medb, also known as Maeve, is a prominent example of a powerful female leader in Celtic mythology. In the Irish epic Táin Bó Cúailnge (The Cattle Raid of Cooley), Medb is depicted as a fierce and ambitious queen who leads her armies into battle. Her character symbolizes female power and authority, challenging the notion that leadership was solely the domain of men.

Beyond mythology, historical accounts also highlight the existence of powerful Celtic queens and female leaders. These women played crucial roles in politics, diplomacy, and decision-making within their communities. Their contributions were instrumental in shaping the social, economic, and cultural fabric of Celtic societies.

7.2.3 Reevaluating Artifacts and Burial Practices

To uncover the hidden histories of Celtic women, it is essential to reevaluate artifacts and burial practices through a gender-inclusive lens. Traditionally, archaeological interpretations have often assumed that certain artifacts or burial sites belonged exclusively to men, disregarding the possibility of women's involvement. However, recent studies have challenged these assumptions and revealed a more nuanced understanding of gender roles in Celtic societies.

For instance, the discovery of weapons buried with women suggests their active participation in warfare. These findings indicate that women were not merely passive observers or victims of conflict but actively engaged in battle. Similarly, the analysis of burial practices has revealed the presence of high-status women buried with symbols of power and authority, further emphasizing their significant roles in Celtic society.

7.2.4 The Impact of Unveiling Hidden Histories

The rediscovery of women's stories and contributions in Celtic societies has profound implications for our understanding of history and the role of women in ancient cultures. By challenging patriarchal biases and acknowledging the diverse roles of women, we can create a more accurate and inclusive narrative of the past.

Unveiling the hidden histories of Celtic women also has a broader impact on contemporary society. It provides inspiration and empowerment for women today, demonstrating that they have always been capable of leadership, courage, and agency. By recognizing the historical legacy of women warriors and leaders, we can challenge gender stereotypes and promote gender equality in our own time.

Conclusion

Rediscovering the stories and contributions of women in Celtic societies is a crucial step in challenging patriarchal biases and unveiling hidden histories. By reevaluating artifacts, burial practices, and historical accounts, we can shed light on the participation of women in warfare and their positions of power and authority. This rediscovery not only enriches our understanding of Celtic cultures but also inspires and empowers women today.

By recognizing the importance of gender fluidity and inclusivity, we can create a more equitable and just society for all.

7.3 Reevaluating Artifacts and Burial Practices

Artifacts and burial practices provide valuable insights into the lives and roles of individuals in ancient societies. However, the interpretation of these artifacts and burial practices has often been influenced by patriarchal biases, leading to a limited understanding of the roles and contributions of women in Celtic societies. In order to unveil the hidden histories of warrior women in the Celts, it is crucial to reevaluate these artifacts and burial practices through a more inclusive and gender-sensitive lens.

7.3.1 Artifacts as Clues to Women's Participation in Warfare

Archaeological excavations have unearthed a wide range of artifacts that suggest the active participation of women in warfare in Celtic societies. Weapons such as swords, spears, and shields have been discovered in female burials, indicating that women were not only associated with warfare but also actively engaged in combat. These findings challenge the traditional notion that women were solely confined to domestic roles and were passive participants in Celtic society.

Furthermore, the presence of defensive armor, such as chainmail, in female burials suggests that women were not only involved in battles but also played significant roles in the defense of their communities. These artifacts provide tangible evidence of the physical strength and combat skills possessed by Celtic women, challenging the patriarchal biases that have historically downplayed their contributions.

7.3.2 Burial Practices as Indicators of Women's Status and Authority

Burial practices also offer valuable insights into the status and authority held by women in Celtic societies. The presence of elaborate grave goods, such as jewelry, mirrors, and chariots, in female burials suggests that women held positions of power and prestige. These grave goods not only symbolize wealth but also indicate the social standing and influence of women in their communities.

Additionally, the positioning of burials within sacred landscapes and the construction of elaborate burial mounds for women further emphasize their importance and significance. These burial practices highlight the reverence and respect accorded to women in Celtic societies, challenging the notion that they were marginalized or excluded from positions of authority.

7.3.3 Symbolism and Rituals in Burial Practices

The symbolism and rituals associated with burial practices also shed light on the roles and identities of women in Celtic societies. The presence of weapons and armor in female burials suggests that women were not only warriors but also revered as protectors and defenders of their communities. This challenges the patriarchal bias that associates warfare solely with masculinity and highlights the multifaceted nature of gender roles in Celtic cultures.

Furthermore, the inclusion of personal items and symbols

associated with female deities in female burials suggests a connection between women and the divine. The Morrígan, a prominent Celtic goddess of war and battle, is often depicted as a powerful and fierce figure. The presence of artifacts associated with the Morrígan in female burials suggests that women were not only inspired by these mythological figures but also sought to embody their qualities of strength and courage.

7.3.4 Unveiling Hidden Histories through Reevaluation

Reevaluating artifacts and burial practices through a more inclusive lens allows us to uncover the hidden histories of warrior women in Celtic societies. By challenging patriarchal biases and acknowledging the active participation of women in warfare, we can paint a more accurate and comprehensive picture of Celtic society.

This reevaluation also highlights the need for a more nuanced understanding of gender roles and fluidity in Celtic cultures. The presence of women in positions of power and authority, as evidenced by burial practices, challenges the notion of a strictly patriarchal society. It suggests that gender roles in Celtic societies were more fluid and that women had agency and influence in various aspects of life, including warfare.

By reevaluating artifacts and burial practices, we can begin to dismantle the patriarchal lens through which history and archaeology have often been written. This allows us to recognize and celebrate the diverse contributions of women in Celtic societies, providing a more accurate and inclusive narrative of their history.

The reevaluation of artifacts and burial practices not only enriches our understanding of the past but also has important implications for the present. It challenges the prevailing patriarchal biases that have marginalized and silenced women's voices throughout history. By acknowledging the roles and contributions of warrior women in Celtic societies, we can inspire and empower women today, encouraging them to embrace their own strength and agency.

In conclusion, reevaluating artifacts and burial practices is crucial in unveiling the hidden histories of warrior women in Celtic societies. By challenging patriarchal biases and recognizing the active participation of women in warfare, we can paint a more accurate and inclusive picture of Celtic society. This reevaluation also highlights the importance of gender fluidity and the need for a more nuanced understanding of gender roles in Celtic cultures. By embracing these insights, we can celebrate the diverse contributions of women in Celtic societies and inspire future generations to challenge gender stereotypes and pursue their own paths of strength and empowerment.

7.4 Impact of Unveiling Hidden Histories

The unveiling of hidden histories surrounding the roles of women in Celtic societies has had a profound impact on our understanding of the past. By challenging patriarchal biases and reevaluating historical and archaeological evidence, we have begun to uncover the significant contributions of women, particularly in the realms of warfare and leadership. This newfound knowledge not only reshapes our understanding of Celtic societies but also has broader implications for our understanding of gender roles and the importance of gender fluidity in cultures throughout history.

7.4.1 Redefining Celtic Societies

The revelation of women's participation in warfare and positions of power in Celtic societies challenges the traditional narrative that has often portrayed these societies as strictly patriarchal. By uncovering the stories of female warriors such as Boudica and Queen Medb, we are forced to reassess our understanding of Celtic societies as more egalitarian and inclusive than previously believed. This redefinition not only provides a more accurate representation of the past but also challenges the biases that have shaped historical and archaeological research.

7.4.2 Empowering Women's Narratives

The unveiling of hidden histories empowers women's narratives and gives voice to the experiences and contributions of Celtic women. By highlighting the stories of female warriors and leaders, we are able to challenge the dominant patriarchal lens through which history has often been written. This shift in perspective allows us to recognize the agency and power of women in Celtic societies and provides a more balanced and inclusive understanding of the past.

7.4.3 Challenging Stereotypes and Misconceptions

The discovery of evidence suggesting women's participation in warfare and positions of authority challenges long-held stereotypes and misconceptions about gender roles in Celtic societies. The prevailing assumption that women were solely confined to domestic and reproductive roles is proven to be incomplete and inaccurate. By acknowledging the diverse roles and capabilities of Celtic women, we challenge the notion that women's contributions were limited to the private sphere and highlight the complexity and diversity of Celtic societies.

7.4.4 Inspiring Gender Fluidity and Social Acceptance

The recognition of gender fluidity in Celtic cultures has significant implications for contemporary society. By acknowledging the acceptance and fluidity of gender roles in Celtic societies, we challenge the rigid binary understanding of gender that has dominated Western cultures for centuries. The cultural significance of gender fluidity in Celtic societies serves as a powerful reminder that gender is not fixed but rather a social construct that can vary across different cultures and historical periods. This understanding can inspire greater acceptance and inclusivity in modern society, allowing individuals to express their gender identity authentically.

7.4.5 Reevaluating Historical and Archaeological Research

The unveiling of hidden histories necessitates a reevaluation of historical and archaeological research methodologies. The biases that have shaped the interpretation of artifacts, burial practices, and historical accounts must be critically examined and challenged. By recognizing the potential for patriarchal biases to downplay or ignore the roles of women in Celtic societies, we can strive for a more inclusive and accurate understanding of the past. This reevaluation also highlights the importance of diverse perspectives and interdisciplinary approaches in historical and archaeological research.

7.4.6 Cultural Significance and Legacy

The impact of unveiling hidden histories extends beyond academia and has cultural significance for Celtic communities and the broader public. By recognizing and celebrating the contributions of women in Celtic societies, we honor their legacy and challenge the erasure of their stories. This recognition also provides a source of inspiration for contemporary women, highlighting the strength, resilience, and leadership capabilities of their Celtic ancestors. The cultural significance of unveiling hidden histories lies in the empowerment and validation it offers to women, fostering a sense of pride and connection to their heritage.

In conclusion, the unveiling of hidden histories surrounding the roles of women in Celtic societies has had a profound impact on our understanding of the past. By challenging patriarchal biases and reevaluating historical and archaeological evidence, we have begun to recognize the significant contributions of women in warfare and positions of power. This redefinition of Celtic societies empowers women's narratives, challenges stereotypes, and inspires a greater acceptance of gender fluidity. The impact of unveiling hidden histories extends beyond academia, providing cultural significance and honoring the legacy of Celtic women. By continuing to explore and celebrate the stories of warrior women and female leaders, we ensure that their contributions are not forgotten and that the conversation surrounding gender roles in Celtic societies continues to evolve.

Chapter 8

Gender Fluidity in Celtic Cultures

8.1 Understanding Gender Fluidity in Celtic Societies

Gender fluidity refers to the concept that gender is not fixed and can change over time or in different contexts. In Celtic societies, there was a recognition and acceptance of gender fluidity that differed from the rigid gender roles found in many other ancient cultures. This understanding of gender fluidity played a significant role in shaping the roles and expectations of individuals within Celtic communities.

8.1.1 Fluidity in Gender Roles

Celtic societies had a more flexible approach to gender roles compared to other ancient civilizations. While there were certain expectations and responsibilities associated with being male or female, these roles were not strictly defined or limited. Celtic cultures recognized that individuals could possess qualities and abilities traditionally associated with both genders, and this fluidity was accepted and even celebrated.

In Celtic societies, individuals were not confined to predetermined gender roles based solely on their biological sex. Instead, they were allowed to express themselves and pursue activities and roles that aligned with their personal strengths and interests. This fluidity extended beyond the binary understanding of gender, allowing for a more nuanced and inclusive perspective.

8.1.2 Gender Fluidity in Celtic Mythology

Celtic mythology provides further evidence of the acceptance of gender fluidity within Celtic societies. The Morrígan, for example, was a prominent goddess associated with war and battle. She was often depicted as a shapeshifter, assuming different forms and genders depending on the situation. This fluidity in gender representation within mythology reflects the broader acceptance of gender fluidity in Celtic cultures.

Other female figures in Celtic mythology, such as Macha and Scáthach, also challenge traditional gender roles. Macha was a warrior queen who possessed great strength and leadership qualities. Scáthach, on the other hand, was a renowned warrior and teacher who trained legendary heroes. These mythological figures demonstrate that women in Celtic societies were not limited to passive or domestic roles but could actively participate in warfare and hold positions of power.

8.1.3 Social Acceptance of Gender Fluidity

The acceptance of gender fluidity in Celtic societies had a profound impact on social dynamics and the treatment of individuals. Unlike many other ancient cultures, where strict gender roles often led to the marginalization or oppression of certain groups, Celtic societies allowed for a more inclusive and egalitarian approach.

The fluidity in gender roles meant that individuals were not confined to predetermined expectations based on their sex. This allowed for greater freedom of expression and the ability to pursue roles and activities that aligned with their personal strengths and interests. It also fostered a more inclusive and accepting society, where individuals were valued for their abilities and contributions rather than being limited by their gender.

8.1.4 Cultural Significance of Gender Fluidity

The recognition and acceptance of gender fluidity in Celtic societies had a profound cultural significance. It challenged the patriarchal norms prevalent in many other ancient civilizations and provided a more egalitarian framework for social organization. This cultural acceptance of gender fluidity allowed for a more diverse and inclusive society, where individuals were valued for their unique qualities and contributions.

The fluidity in gender roles also contributed to the strength and resilience of Celtic communities. By allowing individuals to pursue roles and activities that aligned with their strengths and interests, Celtic societies were able to harness the full potential of their members. This inclusivity and recognition of diverse talents and abilities fostered a sense of unity and cooperation within Celtic communities.

Furthermore, the cultural significance of gender fluidity in Celtic societies extends beyond the ancient world. It serves as a reminder of the importance of embracing diversity and challenging rigid gender norms in modern society. By understanding and appreciating the fluidity of gender, we can create a more inclusive and equitable world where individuals are free to express themselves and pursue their passions without fear of judgment or discrimination.

In conclusion, gender fluidity played a significant role in shaping the roles and expectations of individuals within Celtic societies. The acceptance of gender fluidity challenged traditional gender roles and allowed individuals to express themselves and pursue activities and roles that aligned with their personal strengths and interests. This fluidity is evident in Celtic mythology, where female figures associated with war and battle challenge traditional gender roles. The social acceptance of gender fluidity in Celtic societies fostered a more inclusive and egalitarian society, where individuals were valued for their abilities and contributions rather than being limited by their gender. The cultural significance of gender fluidity in Celtic societies serves as a reminder of the importance of embracing diversity and challenging rigid gender norms in modern society.

8.2 The Role of Gender Fluidity in Celtic Mythology

Celtic mythology is rich with stories and legends that provide insights into the cultural beliefs and values of the ancient Celts. One fascinating aspect of Celtic mythology is the presence of gender fluidity, which challenges traditional notions of gender roles and highlights the diverse expressions of identity within Celtic societies. This section will explore the role of gender fluidity in Celtic mythology and its significance in understanding the complexities of Celtic culture.

8.2.1 Fluidity in Divine Beings

In Celtic mythology, the divine beings often exhibited fluidity in their gender identities. The Morrígan, for example, is a prominent figure associated with war and battle. She is depicted as a triad of goddesses, each representing different aspects of war. The Morrígan's ability to shift between forms and genders reflects the fluid nature of gender in Celtic mythology. This fluidity challenges the binary understanding of gender and suggests a more nuanced understanding of identity within Celtic societies.

Other Celtic deities, such as Manannán mac Lir and Cú Chulainn, also display fluidity in their gender identities. Manannán mac Lir, the god of the sea, is known to transform into both male and female forms. Cú Chulainn, a legendary hero, is said to have taken on female roles during his training. These examples demonstrate that gender fluidity was not only accepted but also celebrated within Celtic mythology.

8.2.2 Symbolism and Representation

The presence of gender fluidity in Celtic mythology serves as a powerful symbol of the interconnectedness and fluidity of all aspects of life. It challenges the rigid gender roles imposed by patriarchal societies and highlights the importance of embracing diversity and individual expression. The ability of divine beings to transcend traditional gender boundaries suggests a deep respect for the fluidity of human identity.

Furthermore, the representation of gender fluidity in Celtic mythology provides a counter-narrative to the patriarchal lens through which history and archaeology have often been written. By acknowledging and exploring the fluidity of gender in Celtic mythology, we can begin to challenge the biases that have downplayed or ignored the different roles of women in Celtic societies.

8.2.3 Mythological Tales and Gender Fluidity

Many mythological tales in Celtic folklore feature characters who challenge traditional gender norms and exhibit gender fluidity. These stories often depict women who take on traditionally masculine roles, such as warriors and leaders. The tale of Queen Medb (Maeve) in the epic Táin Bó Cúailnge (The Cattle Raid of Cooley) is a prime example.

Queen Medb is portrayed as a powerful and assertive ruler who leads her armies into battle. She defies societal expectations of women and demonstrates that gender does not limit one's ability to lead and fight. Medb's story highlights the fluidity of gender roles within Celtic mythology and challenges the notion that women were solely confined to domestic spheres.

8.2.4 Lessons from Gender Fluidity

The presence of gender fluidity in Celtic mythology offers valuable lessons for modern society. It encourages us to question and challenge the rigid gender norms that persist today. By embracing the fluidity of gender, we can create a more inclusive and accepting society that celebrates the diversity of human experiences.

Furthermore, understanding the cultural significance of gender fluidity in Celtic mythology allows us to reevaluate historical and archaeological evidence through a more inclusive lens. By acknowledging the existence and contributions of women in Celtic societies, we can uncover hidden histories and challenge patriarchal biases that have shaped our understanding of the past.

In conclusion, gender fluidity plays a significant role in Celtic mythology, challenging traditional gender roles and highlighting the diversity of human identity. The fluidity exhibited by divine beings and the representation of gender non-conforming characters in mythological tales provide valuable insights into the complexities of Celtic culture. By recognizing and embracing gender fluidity, we can learn important lessons about acceptance, inclusivity, and the need to challenge patriarchal biases in our own society.

8.3 Gender Fluidity and Social Acceptance

Gender fluidity refers to the concept that gender is not fixed and can change over time or in different contexts. In Celtic societies, gender fluidity was not only accepted but also celebrated. The fluidity of gender roles and identities played a significant role in shaping the social dynamics and cultural practices of the Celts. This chapter explores the concept of gender fluidity in Celtic cultures and its impact on social acceptance.

8.3.1 Fluidity in Gender Roles

Celtic societies had a more flexible approach to gender roles compared to many other ancient civilizations. The roles and responsibilities assigned to individuals were not solely determined by their biological sex but were influenced by their abilities, skills, and personal inclinations. This fluidity allowed individuals to move between different gender roles and occupations based on their strengths and interests.

In Celtic communities, both men and women had the freedom to engage in various activities traditionally associated with the opposite gender. Women were not confined to domestic roles but actively participated in public life, including warfare, politics, and economic activities. Similarly, men were not limited to the role of warriors but also engaged in artistic pursuits, craftsmanship, and other traditionally feminine domains.

8.3.2 Gender Fluidity in Celtic Mythology

Celtic mythology provides further evidence of the acceptance of gender fluidity in Celtic cultures. Many mythological tales feature characters who challenge traditional gender norms and exhibit fluid gender identities. The Morrígan, for example, is a prominent Celtic goddess associated with war and battle. She is often depicted as a shapeshifter, assuming both male and female forms. This fluidity in gender representation reflects the Celtic belief in the interconnectedness and fluidity of all aspects of life, including gender.

Other female figures in Celtic mythology, such as Macha and Scáthach, also defy traditional gender roles. Macha is a goddess associated with sovereignty and fertility, but she is also depicted as a powerful warrior. Scáthach, on the other hand, is a legendary warrior woman who trains the hero Cú Chulainn in the art of combat. These mythological narratives not only challenge gender stereotypes but also highlight the valued contributions of women in warfare and leadership.

8.3.3 Social Acceptance of Gender Fluidity

The acceptance of gender fluidity in Celtic societies extended beyond mythology and permeated everyday life. Historical accounts and archaeological evidence suggest that Celtic women actively participated in warfare and held positions of authority. The social acceptance of gender fluidity allowed women to break free from traditional gender constraints and pursue roles traditionally reserved for men.

In Celtic societies, women warriors, known as "bandraoi" or "warrior women," were respected and admired for their bravery and skill in battle. They fought alongside men, defending their communities and asserting their power. The presence of female warriors in Celtic armies challenges the notion that women were passive and confined to domestic roles.

Furthermore, Celtic women held positions of authority and leadership in both mythological and historical contexts. Queen Medb (Maeve) of Connacht, for instance, is a prominent figure in Irish mythology and is depicted as a powerful and influential ruler. She led her armies into battle and was known for her strategic prowess. Medb's portrayal as a strong and capable leader reflects the social acceptance of women in positions of power in Celtic societies.

8.3.4 Cultural Significance of Gender Fluidity

The fluidity of gender roles and the acceptance of gender diversity had profound cultural significance in Celtic societies. It fostered a sense of equality and inclusivity, allowing individuals to express their authentic selves without fear of judgment or discrimination. This cultural acceptance of gender fluidity contributed to the overall social cohesion and harmony within Celtic communities.

The celebration of gender fluidity also had implications for the understanding of power dynamics. By recognizing and valuing the contributions of women in traditionally male-dominated spheres, Celtic societies challenged patriarchal norms and created a more balanced and equitable society. This cultural acceptance of gender fluidity served as a powerful tool for challenging patriarchal biases and dismantling gender-based hierarchies.

The cultural significance of gender fluidity in Celtic societies extends beyond the ancient world. It offers valuable lessons for modern society, where gender norms and expectations continue to limit individuals' freedom and self-expression. By embracing the fluidity of gender roles and identities, we can create a more inclusive and accepting society that celebrates the diversity of human experiences.

In conclusion, gender fluidity was an integral part of Celtic cultures, allowing individuals to move between different gender roles and occupations based on their abilities and interests. This fluidity is evident in Celtic mythology, where characters challenge traditional gender norms. The social acceptance of gender fluidity in Celtic societies enabled women to actively participate in warfare and hold positions of authority. The cultural significance of gender fluidity lies in its ability to challenge patriarchal biases and create a more inclusive and equitable society. By embracing the lessons from Celtic cultures, we can strive for a future where gender fluidity is celebrated and social acceptance is the norm.

8.4 Lessons from Celtic Cultures for Modern Society

Celtic cultures offer valuable lessons for modern society, particularly in relation to gender fluidity and the recognition of women's contributions. By examining the historical and mythological evidence of Celtic societies, we can challenge patriarchal biases and unveil hidden histories that have often downplayed or ignored the roles of women. These lessons can inspire us to reevaluate our own societal norms and strive for greater gender equality and acceptance.

8.4.1 Embracing Gender Fluidity

One of the most striking aspects of Celtic cultures is their acceptance of gender fluidity. In Celtic societies, gender was not strictly binary, and individuals were not confined to rigid gender roles. This fluidity is evident in both historical accounts and mythological tales, where we find examples of women warriors, female leaders, and individuals who transcended traditional gender norms.

By exploring the role of gender fluidity in Celtic societies, we can challenge the notion that gender is fixed and immutable. This understanding can help us break free from the constraints of gender stereotypes and create a more inclusive and accepting society. It teaches us that gender should not be a barrier to pursuing our passions, ambitions, or leadership roles.

8.4.2 Recognizing Women's Contributions

The stories of Celtic warrior women and female leaders serve as a powerful reminder of the significant contributions women have made throughout history. By shedding light on these hidden histories, we can challenge the patriarchal lens through which history and archaeology have often been written.

Celtic societies provide evidence that women not only participated in warfare but also held positions of power and authority. Figures like Boudica and Queen Medb demonstrate the leadership and military prowess of Celtic women. Additionally, Celtic mythology is replete with female figures associated with war and battle, such as the Morrígan and other warrior goddesses.

By recognizing and celebrating the achievements of women in Celtic societies, we can inspire and empower women in our own time. These stories serve as a reminder that women have always been capable of greatness and deserve equal recognition and opportunities.

8.4.3 Challenging Gender Stereotypes

The evidence of women's participation in warfare and positions of authority in Celtic societies challenges long-held gender stereotypes. It forces us to question the assumptions and biases that have shaped our understanding of history and archaeology.

By challenging these stereotypes, we can create a more inclusive and accurate narrative of the past. This, in turn, can help dismantle the barriers that prevent women from fully participating in all aspects of society today. It encourages us to question the limitations placed on women and to recognize their potential for leadership, strength, and courage.

8.4.4 Cultural Significance

The lessons from Celtic cultures have cultural significance that extends beyond gender equality. By exploring the rich tapestry of Celtic societies, we gain a deeper understanding of the diversity and complexity of human experiences.

Celtic cultures teach us the importance of embracing different perspectives and valuing the contributions of all individuals, regardless of gender. They remind us that history is not a monolithic narrative but a tapestry woven from the stories of diverse individuals.

By embracing the cultural significance of Celtic societies, we can foster a more inclusive and pluralistic society. We can learn to appreciate and celebrate the richness of our collective heritage, recognizing the contributions of all individuals, regardless of their gender or other social identities.

In conclusion, the lessons from Celtic cultures provide valuable insights for modern society. By embracing gender fluidity, recognizing women's contributions, challenging gender stereotypes, and appreciating the cultural significance of diverse narratives, we can create a more inclusive and equitable world. The stories of Celtic warrior women and female leaders inspire us to challenge patriarchal biases and strive for greater gender equality. Let us learn from the past and work towards a future where all individuals are valued and empowered, regardless of their gender.

9

Chapter 9

The Influence of Celtic Warrior Women

9.1 Inspiration for Modern Women

Throughout history, women have often been marginalized and their contributions overlooked. However, the stories of Celtic warrior women provide inspiration and empowerment for modern women seeking to challenge societal norms and break free from gender stereotypes. The tales of these fierce and courageous women serve as a reminder that women have always been capable of strength, leadership, and bravery.

The stories of Boudica (Boadicea) and Queen Medb (Maeve) are particularly inspiring. Boudica, the warrior queen of the Iceni tribe, led a rebellion against the Roman Empire in 60-61 AD. Despite facing overwhelming odds, she fearlessly fought for the freedom of her people and became a symbol of resistance against oppression. Boudica's unwavering determination and her refusal to accept defeat serve as a powerful example for modern women facing their own battles.

Similarly, Queen Medb, a legendary figure in Irish mythology, is renowned for her strength and assertiveness. In the epic tale of Táin Bó Cúailnge (The Cattle Raid of Cooley), Medb leads her army in a quest to obtain the prized bull of Cooley. Her strategic prowess and leadership skills are evident as she navigates through various challenges and obstacles. Medb's story reminds us that women have always possessed the ability to lead and excel in positions of power.

Celtic mythology is also rich with female figures associated with war and battle. The Morrígan, the goddess of war and battle, is a prime example. She is often depicted as a fierce and formidable figure, capable of shaping the outcome of battles. Other warrior goddesses, such as Macha and Badb, also play significant roles in Celtic mythology. These powerful female figures challenge the notion that women are inherently passive or weak, and instead highlight their strength and resilience.

The influence of Celtic warrior women extends beyond their individual stories. Their existence challenges the patriarchal lens through which history and archaeology have often been written. For centuries, women's roles and contributions have been downplayed or ignored, perpetuating the belief that women were primarily confined to domestic spheres. However, the evidence suggests that Celtic women did participate in warfare and held positions of authority.

Archaeological discoveries, such as the burial sites of warrior women, provide tangible proof of their existence and involvement in combat. The presence of weapons and armor in these burials indicates that these women were not merely passive observers but active participants in battle. Additionally, historical accounts and ancient texts mention the involvement of women in Celtic armies and their contributions to battle strategies.

The importance of gender fluidity in Celtic cultures cannot be overlooked. Celtic societies recognized and accepted a more fluid understanding of gender roles, allowing for greater freedom and agency for individuals. This acceptance of gender fluidity allowed women to step outside traditional gender norms and pursue roles traditionally reserved for men, such as warriors and leaders. The cultural significance of this acceptance is profound, as it challenges the rigid gender binaries that have often limited women's opportunities and potential.

For modern women, the stories of Celtic warrior women serve as a reminder that they too can defy societal expectations and pursue their dreams and ambitions. These stories inspire women to embrace their own strength, courage, and leadership abilities. They encourage women to challenge the status quo, break free from gender stereotypes, and strive for equality and empowerment.

In conclusion, the influence of Celtic warrior women is far-reaching and continues to inspire modern women. Their stories provide a powerful reminder that women have always possessed the strength, resilience, and leadership qualities necessary to shape their own destinies. By embracing the lessons from Celtic cultures and challenging patriarchal biases, women can continue to pave the way for a more inclusive and equal society. The legacy of Celtic warrior women serves as a testament to the indomitable spirit of women throughout history and their ability to overcome adversity.

9.2 Impact on Feminist Movements

The stories and legacies of Celtic warrior women have had a profound impact on feminist movements throughout history. These powerful and resilient women have served as inspiration and role models for generations of women seeking to challenge patriarchal norms and fight for gender equality. Their stories have not only shed light on the hidden histories of women in Celtic societies but have also provided a framework for understanding the potential and capabilities of women in all aspects of life.

9.2.1 Empowerment and Liberation

The tales of Celtic warrior women, such as Boudica and Queen Medb, have been instrumental in empowering women and encouraging them to break free from societal constraints. These women defied traditional gender roles and expectations, demonstrating that women were just as capable as men in leadership, warfare, and decision-making. Their stories have served as a rallying cry for women seeking liberation from oppressive systems and have inspired countless individuals to challenge the status quo.

The courage and resilience displayed by these warrior women have become symbols of female empowerment. Their refusal to be silenced or marginalized has resonated with feminist movements, encouraging women to reclaim their voices and assert their rights. The stories of these women have reminded women that they have the strength and capability to overcome any obstacle and make a significant impact on society.

9.2.2 Challenging Gender Stereotypes

The existence of Celtic warrior women has challenged deeply ingrained gender stereotypes that have limited women's roles throughout history. By showcasing women who were skilled warriors, leaders, and strategists, these stories have shattered the notion that women are inherently weak or incapable of participating in traditionally male-dominated spheres.

The representation of women as warriors in Celtic mythology and history has provided a counter-narrative to the patriarchal lens through which history and archaeology have often been written. It has forced scholars and researchers to reevaluate their assumptions and acknowledge the diverse roles that women played in Celtic societies. This reevaluation has had a ripple effect on feminist movements, encouraging a reexamination of gender roles and the recognition of women's contributions in other cultures and time periods.

9.2.3 Inspiring Activism and Advocacy

The stories of Celtic warrior women have not only inspired individuals but have also fueled activism and advocacy for women's rights. These women have become symbols of resistance and strength, motivating women to fight for their rights and challenge the systemic barriers that limit their opportunities.

The recognition of Celtic warrior women has also led to increased representation of women in historical narratives and popular culture. Their stories have been retold in books, films, and other forms of media, bringing their achievements to a wider audience. This increased visibility has helped to normalize the idea of women in positions of power and authority, inspiring future generations of women to pursue their ambitions without fear or hesitation.

9.2.4 Redefining Femininity and Gender Roles

The stories of Celtic warrior women have challenged traditional notions of femininity and gender roles. These women defied societal expectations by embracing their strength, courage, and assertiveness. By doing so, they have expanded the definition of femininity and demonstrated that there is no one way to be a woman.

The cultural significance of gender fluidity in Celtic societies has also played a role in redefining gender roles. The acceptance and celebration of individuals who did not conform to traditional gender norms have provided a historical precedent for the recognition and inclusion of diverse gender identities in modern society. The stories of Celtic warrior women have highlighted the fluidity of gender in Celtic cultures, emphasizing the importance of embracing and respecting individuals' self-identified gender identities.

In conclusion, the impact of Celtic warrior women on feminist movements cannot be overstated. Their stories have empowered women, challenged gender stereotypes, inspired activism, and redefined femininity and gender roles. By recognizing and celebrating the achievements of these remarkable women, we not only honor their legacies but also pave the way for a more inclusive and equal society. The lessons learned from Celtic cultures, particularly the importance of gender fluidity, continue to resonate with modern society, reminding us of the power and potential of women in all aspects of life.

9.3 Cultural and Historical Legacy

The cultural and historical legacy of Celtic warrior women is a testament to the strength, resilience, and power of women in Celtic societies. Throughout this book, we have explored the stories of remarkable women such as Boudica and Queen Medb, as well as the rich tapestry of female figures in Celtic mythology. These women have left an indelible mark on history and continue to inspire and empower women today.

9.3.1 Breaking Gender Stereotypes

The legacy of Celtic warrior women challenges traditional gender stereotypes and highlights the complexity of gender roles in Celtic societies. The evidence we have uncovered throughout this book suggests that Celtic women not only participated in warfare but also held positions of power and authority. This challenges the patriarchal lens through which history and archaeology have often been written, which has downplayed or ignored the different roles of women in Celtic societies.

9.3.2 Women in Positions of Authority

The stories of Boudica and Queen Medb demonstrate that women in Celtic societies could rise to positions of leadership and command. Boudica, as a warrior queen, led her people in a fierce rebellion against Roman rule, while Queen Medb's role in the Táin Bó Cúailnge showcased her authority and strategic prowess. These women were not anomalies but rather examples of the broader societal acceptance of women in positions of power.

9.3.3 Cultural Significance

The cultural significance of Celtic warrior women cannot be overstated. These women were not only respected for their military prowess but also revered as symbols of female power and authority. In Celtic mythology, figures such as the Morrígan embodied the strength and ferocity of battle. Their stories and representations in art and literature served as inspiration for generations of Celtic women, reinforcing the idea that women were capable of great feats and deserving of respect and recognition.

9.3.4 Inspiring Modern Women

The legacy of Celtic warrior women continues to inspire and empower modern women. Their stories serve as a reminder that women have always been capable of extraordinary achievements, even in societies that may have been patriarchal in nature. By reclaiming and celebrating the stories of these women, we can challenge the limitations imposed by gender norms and encourage women to pursue their ambitions and dreams without fear or hesitation.

9.3.5 Impact on Feminist Movements

The stories of Celtic warrior women have had a profound impact on feminist movements. By highlighting the historical and cultural legacy of these women, feminist scholars and activists have been able to challenge the dominant narrative that women's contributions have been secondary or insignificant. The recognition of Celtic warrior women as powerful and influential figures in history has helped to reshape the understanding of women's roles and capabilities, both in the past and in the present.

9.3.6 Rediscovering Hidden Histories

The exploration of Celtic warrior women has also led to a reevaluation of historical artifacts and burial practices. By examining these sources through a gender-inclusive lens, researchers have been able to uncover previously overlooked evidence of women's participation in warfare and positions of authority. This rediscovery of hidden histories has not only enriched our understanding of Celtic societies but has also challenged the biases and assumptions that have shaped historical and archaeological research.

9.3.7 Lessons for Modern Society

The importance of gender fluidity in Celtic cultures cannot be ignored. The acceptance and recognition of diverse gender identities and expressions in Celtic societies provide valuable lessons for modern society. By embracing gender fluidity, Celtic cultures created space for individuals to explore and express their true selves, free from the constraints of rigid gender norms. This inclusivity and acceptance can serve as a model for contemporary society, encouraging us to challenge binary notions of gender and embrace the diversity of human experiences.

9.3.8 Preserving and Celebrating Heritage

The cultural and historical legacy of Celtic warrior women must be preserved and celebrated. By acknowledging and honoring the contributions of these women, we can ensure that their stories are not forgotten or erased. This can be achieved through continued research, education, and the promotion of gender equality. By recognizing the achievements of Celtic warrior women, we can inspire future generations to challenge societal norms and strive for a more inclusive and equitable world.

In conclusion, the cultural and historical legacy of Celtic warrior women is a testament to the strength, resilience, and power of women in Celtic societies. Their stories challenge gender stereotypes, inspire modern women, and have had a profound impact on feminist movements. By rediscovering hidden histories and embracing gender fluidity, we can learn valuable lessons from Celtic cultures and work towards a more inclusive and equitable society. It is essential that we continue the conversation and further research to ensure that the contributions of Celtic warrior women are recognized and celebrated for generations to come.

9.4 Continuing the Conversation

As we come to the end of our exploration into the world of Celtic warrior women, it is important to acknowledge that this conversation is far from over. The uncovering of hidden histories and the reevaluation of traditional narratives has shed light on the significant roles that women played in Celtic societies. However, there is still much more to discover and understand about the experiences and contributions of these remarkable women.

9.4.1 Expanding the Narrative

One of the key takeaways from our journey through Celtic history and mythology is the need to expand the narrative surrounding women's roles in society. The stories of Boudica, Queen Medb, and the Morrígan have provided us with glimpses into the lives of powerful and influential women. However, it is important to remember that these are just a few examples among many.

There is still much research to be done to uncover the stories of other female warriors and leaders who may have been overlooked or forgotten. By continuing to explore the historical and mythological records, we can bring these women out of the shadows and give them the recognition they deserve.

9.4.2 Amplifying Women's Voices

In order to continue the conversation, it is crucial to amplify the voices of women in Celtic studies. Historically, the patriarchal lens through which history and archaeology have been written has often downplayed or ignored the different roles of women in Celtic societies. By actively seeking out and listening to the perspectives of female scholars and researchers, we can gain a more comprehensive understanding of the contributions and experiences of Celtic women.

Additionally, it is important to encourage and support further research in this field. By providing funding and resources for projects that focus on women in Celtic societies, we can continue to uncover new evidence and challenge existing narratives. This will not only enrich our understanding of the past but also pave the way for a more inclusive and accurate portrayal of Celtic history.

9.4.3 Engaging with Gender Fluidity

Throughout our exploration, we have also touched upon the concept of gender fluidity in Celtic cultures. The acceptance and recognition of diverse gender identities and expressions in Celtic societies offer valuable lessons for modern society. By embracing the fluidity of gender, we can challenge rigid gender norms and create a more inclusive and equitable world.

Continuing the conversation on gender fluidity involves engaging with contemporary discussions and movements that advocate for gender equality and acceptance. By supporting organizations and initiatives that promote gender diversity and inclusivity, we can contribute to the ongoing progress towards a more just and understanding society.

9.4.4 Preserving Cultural Significance

The stories of Celtic warrior women hold immense cultural significance. They not only challenge patriarchal biases but also inspire and empower individuals today. It is crucial to preserve and celebrate this cultural heritage for future generations.

One way to continue the conversation is through education and awareness. By incorporating the stories of Celtic warrior women into school curricula and public discourse, we can ensure that their legacies are not forgotten. Additionally, museums and cultural institutions can play a vital role in showcasing artifacts and exhibits that highlight the contributions of women in Celtic societies.

Furthermore, engaging with Celtic communities and supporting their efforts to preserve their cultural heritage is essential. By collaborating with local historians, archaeologists, and community leaders, we can ensure that the stories of Celtic warrior women are accurately represented and celebrated.

In conclusion, the conversation on Celtic warrior women is far from over. By expanding the narrative, amplifying women's voices, engaging with gender fluidity, and preserving cultural significance, we can continue to uncover the hidden histories and challenge patriarchal biases that have shaped our understanding of Celtic societies. Let us carry this conversation forward, celebrating the strength and resilience of the warrior women of the Celts and drawing inspiration from their stories for a more inclusive and equitable future.

10

Chapter 10

Conclusion

10.1 Recap of Key Findings

Throughout this book, we have explored the fascinating world of Celtic societies and the significant roles that women played within them. Our journey has taken us through the realms of history, mythology, and archaeology, uncovering the hidden stories of warrior women who challenged patriarchal biases and left an indelible mark on Celtic cultures. In this final chapter, we will recap the key findings that have emerged from our exploration, highlighting the importance of recognizing women's contributions, discussing future directions for research, and offering final thoughts and reflections.

One of the most significant findings of our investigation is the existence of prominent female warriors in Celtic societies. We have delved into the lives of remarkable women such as Boudica (Boadicea), the warrior queen who led a valiant rebellion against Roman forces, and Queen Medb (Maeve), a powerful figure in Irish mythology who displayed immense strength and authority. These women, along with other female warriors in Celtic mythology, shattered the notion that warfare was solely the domain of men. Their stories serve as a testament to the courage, skill, and leadership abilities of Celtic women.

In addition to the legendary figures of Boudica and Queen Medb, we have explored the rich tapestry of Celtic mythology, which is replete with female figures associated with war and battle. The Morrígan, a goddess of war and sovereignty, stands as a prime example of the reverence given to powerful women in Celtic myth. Other warrior goddesses and female heroes also feature prominently, further emphasizing the cultural significance of women's roles in Celtic societies.

Moving beyond mythology, we have examined historical accounts and archaeological evidence that support the active participation of women in warfare. These sources reveal the existence of women warriors who fought alongside their male counterparts, displaying remarkable skill and bravery on the battlefield. The presence of weapons, armor, and fortifications associated with women further substantiates their involvement in military activities. By challenging stereotypes and misconceptions, we have shed light on the true extent of women's contributions to Celtic armies and battle strategies.

However, our exploration has not been limited to the realm of warfare. We have also delved into the multifaceted roles that women played in Celtic society beyond the battlefield. Women held positions of power and authority, engaging in politics and leadership roles. They made significant economic contributions, participating in trade and commerce. The cultural significance of women's roles cannot be understated, as they played a vital role in shaping the social fabric of Celtic communities.

Throughout our journey, we have also highlighted the biases that have influenced historical and archaeological research, often downplaying or ignoring the different roles of women in Celtic societies. The patriarchal lens through which history has been written has obscured the contributions of women, leading to an incomplete understanding of Celtic cultures. By unveiling hidden histories and challenging these biases, we have sought to rectify this historical injustice and give voice to the warrior women of the Celts.

Furthermore, we have explored the concept of gender fluidity in Celtic cultures. The acceptance and recognition of gender fluid individuals in Celtic societies provide valuable lessons for modern society. The fluidity of gender roles and the cultural significance attached to it challenge the rigid binary understanding of gender prevalent in many societies today. By embracing gender fluidity, Celtic cultures celebrated the diversity of human experiences and fostered a more inclusive and egalitarian society.

In conclusion, our exploration of warrior women in Celtic societies has revealed a rich tapestry of stories, myths, and historical evidence that challenge patriarchal biases and unveil hidden histories. The key findings of our investigation highlight the active participation of women in warfare, their positions of power and authority, and the cultural significance of gender fluidity. By recognizing and celebrating the contributions of women in Celtic cultures, we can inspire modern women, impact feminist movements, and appreciate the enduring legacy of these remarkable individuals. As we conclude this book, we invite readers to continue the conversation, to delve deeper into the lives of warrior women of the Celts, and to explore the untold stories that lie waiting to be discovered.

10.2 Importance of Recognizing Women's Contributions

Throughout this book, we have explored the rich history of warrior women in Celtic societies, challenging patriarchal biases and unveiling hidden histories. It is crucial to recognize and acknowledge the significant contributions of women in Celtic cultures, particularly in the realms of warfare and positions of power. By doing so, we not only give credit where it is due but also gain a more comprehensive understanding of Celtic societies and their gender dynamics.

10.2.1 Shifting the Narrative

For centuries, the dominant narrative in historical and archaeological research has often overlooked or downplayed the roles of women in Celtic societies. This patriarchal lens has perpetuated the notion that women were primarily confined to domestic and subservient roles, while men were the sole participants in warfare and wielders of power. However, as we have explored in this book, there is ample evidence to suggest that this narrative is far from accurate.

By recognizing and highlighting the contributions of women in Celtic societies, we challenge the traditional narrative and provide a more nuanced understanding of the complex social structures and gender dynamics that existed. This shift in the narrative allows us to appreciate the agency and capabilities of Celtic women, breaking free from the constraints of patriarchal biases.

10.2.2 Women Warriors in Celtic History

The historical accounts and archaeological evidence presented in Chapter 5 have demonstrated the active participation of women in warfare. From the legendary Boudica, who led a formidable rebellion against the Roman Empire, to the mythical Queen Medb, who commanded armies in the epic Táin Bó Cúailnge, Celtic women have left an indelible mark on history.

These women warriors were not anomalies or exceptions; they were part of a broader tradition of female warriors in Celtic societies. The stories of other female figures in Celtic mythology, such as the Morrígan and other warrior goddesses, further emphasize the cultural acceptance and reverence for women in positions of power and authority.

10.2.3 Challenging Stereotypes and Misconceptions

By recognizing women's contributions in warfare and positions of power, we challenge the stereotypes and misconceptions that have been perpetuated throughout history. The notion that women were solely confined to domestic roles not only undermines their agency but also limits our understanding of the diverse roles they played in Celtic societies.

By acknowledging the existence of women warriors and leaders, we break free from the constraints of gender norms and challenge the notion that power and authority are inherently male domains. This recognition allows us to appreciate the complexity and diversity of Celtic societies, where women held positions of influence and actively participated in shaping their communities.

10.2.4 Cultural Significance and Legacy

Recognizing women's contributions in Celtic societies holds immense cultural significance. It allows us to celebrate the achievements and capabilities of Celtic women, providing role models and inspiration for future generations. By acknowledging the historical and mythological figures who defied societal expectations, we honor their legacy and ensure that their stories are not forgotten.

Furthermore, recognizing women's contributions in Celtic societies contributes to a more inclusive and accurate understanding of history. It challenges the dominant narrative that has often marginalized women's roles and perspectives, allowing us to reconstruct a more comprehensive and balanced account of Celtic cultures.

10.2.5 Lessons for Modern Society

The importance of recognizing women's contributions in Celtic societies extends beyond academia and historical research. It offers valuable lessons for modern society, where gender equality and inclusivity remain ongoing struggles. By examining the gender fluidity and acceptance that existed in Celtic cultures, we can challenge the rigid gender norms that persist today.

The recognition of women's contributions in Celtic societies serves as a reminder that gender roles are not fixed or predetermined. It encourages us to question and challenge societal expectations, allowing individuals to embrace their full potential regardless of their gender. By embracing the lessons from Celtic cultures, we can strive towards a more equitable and inclusive society.

In conclusion, recognizing and acknowledging the contributions of women in Celtic societies is of utmost importance. By shifting the narrative, challenging stereotypes, and celebrating their achievements, we gain a more comprehensive understanding of Celtic cultures and their gender dynamics. This recognition not only honors the legacy of warrior women but also offers valuable lessons for modern society. By embracing the gender fluidity and acceptance that existed in Celtic cultures, we can strive towards a more inclusive and equitable future.

10.3 Future Directions for Research

As we conclude our exploration of the warrior women of the Celts, it is important to acknowledge that there is still much to uncover and understand about their roles and contributions in Celtic societies. The research conducted thus far has shed light on the existence of female warriors and powerful women in Celtic history and mythology, but there are still many unanswered questions and avenues for further investigation. In this section, we will discuss some potential future directions for research that can continue to deepen our understanding of the warrior women of the Celts.

10.3.1 Uncovering Hidden Histories

One of the most crucial areas for future research is the continued effort to uncover hidden histories of Celtic women. As we have discussed throughout this book, historical and archaeological research has often been biased towards patriarchal narratives, resulting in the marginalization and erasure of women's contributions. It is essential to challenge these biases and actively seek out evidence of women's roles in warfare, leadership, and other aspects of Celtic society. This can be achieved through a comprehensive reevaluation of existing artifacts, burial practices, and historical accounts, as well as the discovery of new sources and archaeological sites.

10.3.2 Interdisciplinary Approaches

To gain a more comprehensive understanding of the warrior women of the Celts, future research should adopt interdisciplinary approaches. By combining the expertise of historians, archaeologists, anthropologists, linguists, and other relevant fields, we can bring together diverse perspectives and methodologies to analyze and interpret the available evidence. This interdisciplinary collaboration can help bridge gaps in knowledge and provide a more nuanced understanding of the roles and experiences of women in Celtic societies.

10.3.3 Comparative Studies

Comparative studies with other ancient societies can also contribute to our understanding of Celtic warrior women. By examining the roles and status of women in other cultures that existed during the same time period, we can identify commonalities and differences in gender dynamics. This comparative approach can help us contextualize the experiences of Celtic women within a broader historical and cultural framework, providing valuable insights into the unique aspects of Celtic societies.

10.3.4 Analysis of Mythological Texts

Celtic mythology offers a rich source of information about the roles and attributes of female figures associated with war and battle. Future research should delve deeper into the analysis of mythological texts, such as the stories of the Morrígan and other warrior goddesses, to uncover the cultural significance and symbolism attached to these figures. By examining the narratives, symbols, and motifs present in these myths, we can gain a deeper understanding of how Celtic societies perceived and valued female warriors.

10.3.5 Genetic and Isotopic Studies

Advancements in genetic and isotopic analysis techniques offer exciting possibilities for future research on the warrior women of the Celts. By studying ancient DNA and isotopic signatures found in skeletal remains, researchers can gain insights into the biological sex and geographic origins of individuals buried with weapons or in warrior-like contexts. This scientific approach can provide concrete evidence of women's participation in warfare and help challenge any lingering doubts or skepticism regarding their roles.

10.3.6 Oral Traditions and Folklore

Oral traditions and folklore have long been important sources of historical and cultural knowledge in Celtic societies. Future research should explore these rich traditions to uncover stories, songs, and legends that may provide valuable insights into the roles and experiences of warrior women. By engaging with local communities and recording their oral histories, researchers can preserve and analyze this invaluable cultural heritage, shedding further light on the warrior women of the Celts.

10.3.7 Intersectionality and Gender Fluidity

Lastly, future research should continue to explore the intersectionality of gender and other social identities in Celtic societies. By examining how factors such as social class, ethnicity, and age intersected with gender, we can gain a more nuanced understanding of the experiences and roles of warrior women. Additionally, further investigation into the cultural significance of gender fluidity in Celtic societies can provide valuable insights into the acceptance and celebration of diverse gender identities.

In conclusion, the study of the warrior women of the Celts is an ongoing and evolving field of research. By continuing to challenge patriarchal biases, adopting interdisciplinary approaches, and exploring new sources of evidence, we can further illuminate the roles and contributions of women in Celtic societies. The future of research in this area holds great promise for uncovering hidden histories, deepening our understanding of gender dynamics, and celebrating the cultural significance of the warrior women of the Celts.

10.4 Final Thoughts and Reflections

Throughout this book, we have delved into the rich and complex history of Celtic societies and the remarkable women who played significant roles within them. From the warrior queen Boudica to the mythological figure Queen Medb, and the powerful goddesses of Celtic mythology, we have explored the diverse and multifaceted nature of Celtic women's contributions to warfare, leadership, and society as a whole. In this final chapter, we will reflect on the importance of recognizing and celebrating these warrior women, as well as the broader implications of our findings.

10.4.1 Embracing the Complexity

One of the key takeaways from our exploration of Celtic societies is the importance of embracing the complexity of history. The patriarchal lens through which history and archaeology have often been written has led to the downplaying or even erasure of the different roles of women in Celtic societies. However, by examining the available evidence and challenging these biases, we have uncovered a wealth of information that suggests women did indeed participate in warfare and held positions of authority.

10.4.2 Reevaluating the Evidence

The evidence we have examined throughout this book has provided compelling support for the active involvement of Celtic women in warfare. From the accounts of Boudica's military campaigns to the mythological tales featuring warrior goddesses, we have seen a consistent pattern of female warriors and leaders in Celtic societies. Additionally, archaeological discoveries such as grave goods and weaponry have further solidified the presence of women in combat roles.

10.4.3 The Cultural Significance of Warrior Women

The existence of warrior women in Celtic societies holds immense cultural significance. It challenges the traditional gender roles and stereotypes that have been perpetuated throughout history. By recognizing and celebrating the contributions of these women, we not only honor their individual achievements but also reshape our understanding of gender dynamics in ancient societies.

The prominence of female warriors in Celtic mythology also highlights the cultural value placed on female power and authority. The Morrígan and other warrior goddesses were revered and feared, embodying the strength and resilience that Celtic society admired. These mythological figures served as role models for both men and women, emphasizing the importance of female agency and leadership.

10.4.4 Lessons for Modern Society

The exploration of gender fluidity in Celtic cultures offers valuable lessons for modern society. Celtic societies recognized and accepted a fluid understanding of gender, allowing individuals to express themselves beyond traditional binary roles. This acceptance of gender diversity challenges the rigid norms that persist in many societies today and encourages us to embrace a more inclusive and accepting perspective.

Furthermore, the stories of Celtic warrior women serve as inspiration for modern women seeking empowerment and equality. Their courage, resilience, and determination in the face of adversity can inspire us to challenge societal expectations and pursue our own ambitions. By reclaiming and celebrating the stories of these women, we contribute to a more inclusive and accurate historical narrative.

10.4.5 Continuing the Conversation

As we conclude our exploration of warrior women in Celtic societies, it is important to acknowledge that there is still much more to uncover. The field of Celtic studies continues to evolve, and ongoing research and discoveries may shed further light on the roles and contributions of women in these ancient societies. It is crucial that we continue to support and encourage further investigation into this fascinating area of study.

In conclusion, the warrior women of the Celts have left an indelible mark on history and mythology. Their stories challenge patriarchal biases, unveil hidden histories, and inspire us to reevaluate our understanding of gender roles and power dynamics. By recognizing and celebrating the contributions of these remarkable women, we not only honor their legacy but also pave the way for a more inclusive and equitable future.

Recognizing and celebrating the multifaceted contributions of women in Celtic societies is essential for understanding the richness and complexity of their history. By embracing the lessons of gender fluidity and the cultural significance of women's roles, we can challenge patriarchal biases and unveil the hidden histories of warrior women in the Celts, inspiring future generations to embrace their own strength and resilience.

www.ingramcontent.com/pod-product-compliance
Lightning Source LLC
Chambersburg PA
CBHW070903160726
48004CB00003B/1224